W9-DFE-016

To Chris Aiken

Shambhala Publications, Inc.
Horticultural Hall
300 Massachusetts Avenue
Boston, Massachusetts 02115

THE WAY OF MYTH

SHAMBHALA · 25TH · ANNIVERSARY
· 1969–1994 ·

THE WAY
OF MYTH

Talking with Joseph Campbell

FRASER BOA

CONTENTS

THE WAY OF MYTH

INTRODUCTION

W<small>E SAT DOWN</small> together and just talked. It was easy talking with Joe Campbell.

Strictly speaking there were five of us in the room: Joe, Richard—the cameraman—and his assistant, the soundman, and myself. But there was also another presence—the one which had brought us all together. Most often it was silent. But sometimes it spoke with authority.

One morning Joe was explaining the concept of eternity in the field of time. He was concentrating on the image of the bull and the bull sacrifice when suddenly he was abruptly interrupted.

"Damn, we just ran out of film! We'll have to stop and reload."

Joe smiled. "These conversations get into a momentum and then we have to break."

We waited while the cameraman loaded another magazine.

"You know, I'm never even sure when the camera is running." Joe said.

Richard swung the camera around on its tripod till it pointed at the soundman huddled over the recorder.

"Slate it." he said.

"Take twenty-two," came the reply.

They were in sync. We could continue.

And Joe was not unconscious of speaking to that other presence. Using the tricks of a great teacher, he let the historical and the theoretical bump up against his own experience and translated it into a language familiar to us all.

Later, Joe described our talks as "informal conversations conducted in the relaxed mood of an unpretentious interview."

They were also contemplations of a lifetime.

For the filming in Hawaii I rented a suite at the Royal Hawaiian on Waikiki beach not far from Joe's home. It's a grand old hotel with oriental carpets and antique furniture magnificently situated for discreetly affluent holidays but, as I later learned, totally unsuitable for filming motion pictures—it has antiquated electrical wiring.

On the morning of the shoot, the cameraman was on his hands and knees trying to gaffer tape a fuse into a rented transformer box when the phone rang. "If that's him don't bring him up here or we'll never get this damned mess sorted out." he said.

It was Joe. We arranged to meet in the restaurant.

We had coffee by the ocean. A single pink hibiscus centered our table.

"You know Waikiki is not a natural beach." Joe said. "All this sand is transported here from down the coast. Arthur Godfrey used to joke about it."

Out on the beach two young men dressed in blue jeans and bare feet speared last night's litter. Another set out canvas chairs under the palms. A beach bum slept with his blanket pulled over his face. There were no bikinis. They would arrive later.

"Godfrey used to broadcast back to America every morning from this room," Joe continued.

We spoke of Julius Larosa and the Maguire sisters and then of other beaches from Joe's past. Monterey in the early thirties was particularly interesting, as I had once written a thesis on John Steinbeck.

Joe laughed. "You remember the party in *Cannery Row*? That was my birthday party. Even the flagpole sitter was actually there. They used to do that sort of thing back then."

Two sparrows landed on the sand near our table. The female squatted, but the male, as if not trusting her demure invitation, stayed his distance. He circled round while she chirped and flippantly pecked at the sand.

"And Doc Ricketts?" I asked.

Joe paused. "Ed Ricketts was the heart of it all."

Suddenly, there was a wild flurry of wings. The male sparrow had accepted the invitation, and the female was having none of it. She pushed her tail down hard against the sand and drove him back with a series of fierce attacks. Then she sat down innocently and began preening her feathers. The male, as if paralyzed somewhere between his instinctual urge and his fear of another rejection, continued to circle. They repeated the ritual two or three times till finally he puffed his feathers, darted past her sharp beak, and quickly consummated the relationship. Then they flew away.

Joe threw his arms up into the air and laughed. "There, that's the story! That's the *whole* story."

We sat quietly. The surf rolled in under the morning sun with imperturbable serenity.

There were other moments during the filming in which I was moved by exactly where the study of mythology had taken Joseph Campbell. One late afternoon he said, ". . . in my own life I am now looking back and I can tell you that there's a won-

derful moment that comes when you realize, 'I'm not striving for anything.' What
I'm doing now is not a means of achieving
something later. After a certain age,
there's not a future, and suddenly the
present becomes rich and it becomes a
thing in itself which you are now experiencing."

Joseph Campbell died on October 30,
1987.

Fraser Boa

1 · GODS

I HAVE A FRIEND who recently gave me a list of things which let you know you're getting old. One, you sink your teeth into a juicy steak and they stay there; another, the little old lady you're leading across the street is your wife; a third, your back goes out more often than you do. But the real killer is this one. You've got to the top of the ladder and found it's against the wrong wall.

Now, at my stage of life, many of the people I'm meeting have realized that the ladder they've climbed was against the wrong wall. And that's because the goal of life came from a practical intention. How do you make money? What's a good way to make money? What are nice ways to live? They've succeeded that way and found that it doesn't feed the guts.

I'm meeting a lot of people in this condition. I've been lecturing around and about at life-furthering institutes — not to academic groups, but people interested in exploring how life deals with these images we study in college — and I've come across a lot of people, mostly men in middle life, who've had to fight the world and win the race and then ended up with a feeling of, "So what? All you get is a gold medal at the best and what can you do with that thing?" They had not built an inner life.

It's a pitiful thing. Men my own age, retired, sitting around, chewing the fat, trying to keep up their golf game. Imagine in your seventies worrying about your golf score! That's not enough! Life doesn't feel that that's enough, and many of them then sign off — they die. I'm told that the life expectancy of a blue collar worker after retirement is hardly five years. When the body doesn't feel it's got anything to do, it says, "Well, I've got nothing to do, so. . . ." That's the wrong wall, and the only thing a person can do is turn the wall into something transparent by re-reading one's life's aims and goals.

Is that true only for individuals or do you feel our whole society has got the ladder against the wrong wall?

When you look at the popular picture of life in America—what the media presents—it's all wrong wall material. The arts have lost their dynamic and so have become violent.

Take television for example. There are only two themes: violence and sex—the primary biological urges of animals. But the spiritual realizations which come to us through these realms of biological experience are totally missed. You have to go to some of the really great poets and great novelists of today to find people who recognize these things, and their books are not on the best-seller list. People today are rootless. They feel rootless. They feel that their lives are without meaning. One encounters this all over the place, and that's a consequence of having climbed the ladder against the wrong wall.

When Dante in the opening line of the *Divine Comedy* says, "In the middle of the way of our lives, I found myself in a dark, dangerous wood," he's talking about this moment. The moment which occurs in your physical life after you have achieved your goals, when either you are on a launching platform to move into a spiritual life, or else your road is blocked—like going down a ski jump and then, instead of going off into the air, bumping up against the wall. The purpose of the first part of

your life is to give you the experiences out
of which you can draw your spiritual realizations. That's what Dante's talking about
there. And so Virgil, the guide—not a
Christian poet but a pagan poet who cele-
brates the dynamics of the activities of the
body and life experience, not the supernatural but the natural graces—says,
"Okay, go back now through hell." That
is to say, go back through your whole
physical life experience and understand its
spiritual reference, which comes through
the purgatorial and then the heavenly experiences.

We see it in marriage, for instance.
There are two stages. First is what I call
the biological stage, which has to do with
producing and raising children, and the
other is what I would call the alchemical
marriage—realizing the spiritual identity
that the two are somehow one person.
There comes a moment in marriage, if you

live long enough and stay with the game long enough, when you realize that a spiritual marriage has happened, that the two individuals are two aspects of one identity. It is the image of the androgyne, the male/female being. That is the image of what is realized through a marriage. In that mythological reference the two are one. But how many people do you know who, after the children have left the nest, get divorced because they haven't engaged in the second, spiritual marriage. We're not given those lessons now in our educational systems, and we don't know how to handle these situations when they arise. It's a shame.

Joe, would you amplify this concept that mythology images the patterns of life?

Well, my personal attitude toward mythology is that mythology is a function of biology. That is to say, it's an expression in visual dream images of the energies that inform the body.

Think of it this way. Since we are fractions of nature, the energies that inform nature also inform our bodies, and the energies that inform our bodies are the same energies that inform *life*. Inwardly, we experience these energies of nature from the body's impulse system. The impulses come to us through the various organs of the body, which represent different functions of our lives, and, since these functions are basically in conflict with each other, there's a conflict of energies in the body.

Now, images in myths represent the many aspects of this conflict—meeting in conflict, resolution of conflict, and harmonization of conflict. So it is not only the personal life that is rendered in dreams, but on the deeper, what might be called mythic, level of dream, it's the statement of bodily powers which have to be dealt with.

Are you talking about instinct when you speak of body energy?

That's one way to talk about it. But there is another. Imagine that somebody who lives from his head gets the idea, "I'm going to live such and such a life." Then he programs a life for himself based on his rational concepts. But down the road one day his body begins to say, "Oh no! This isn't what I'm made for." Then there's a conflict.

You see, there is a basic distinction to be made between the signals and intentions that come from the rational faculties of the head and those that come from the life energies of the body. Goethe brings this conflict out in *Faust*. In the play, Mephistopheles represents the rational faculties which can carry out the desires of Faust, but the dynamics of Faust's wishes all come from Faust's own life. Mephistopheles can furnish Faust with the means for achieving what he wants, but Mephistopheles cannot determine what Faust is going to want. As soon as Mephistopheles helps Faust achieve one thing, then Faust wants something else. And so Faust runs through the intentions of a lifetime one after another, and Mephistopheles furnishes the mechanism that helps him to achieve them. It happens so fast that Faust runs through the whole aim of life, you might say, in one lifetime. Goethe's central theme is this basic conflict between the dynamics of the intender and the dynamics of the life giver. Mephistopheles and Faust, Lucifer and God, your intellect and the dynamics of your heart, are equivalent images for this conflict. But, and this is an important difference, Lucifer—Satan, as he's also known—puts his own intentions ahead of the intentions of the giver of life and is therefore a frustrating rather than facilitating factor.

There's a wonderful man in Germany now, Karlfried of Graf Dürckheim, who said something about the function of therapy that hit me very strongly. He said that one must learn to become transparent to transcendence. Now, transcendence in the broadest sense refers to those energies that are informing the body, which come from you-don't-know-where. The head, however, independent from these energies, has its own system of thinking that's based on phenomenal experiences, empirical experiences, life intentions and so forth, and life sometimes gets concentrated on these "head" intentions. Then the problem of therapy is to bring the "head" into harmony with the energies that are informing the body, so the transcendent energies can come through. Only when this occurs are you transparent to transcendence. This implies yielding to nature, putting yourself in accord with nature, and, I would say, that is the main aim of most of the mythologies of the world.

This is the secret of the symbol, the spiritual, mythological symbol. The symbol itself must be transparent to transcendence. A god is a personification of an energy, a natural energy, which comes either through the external natural world or from the world of our inner nature. When it comes from the inner world of nature, it appears as the imagery of the dream and then of the myth. The deeper you get, the closer you are to the mythic order; the shallower you get, the closer you are to the "head" order.

As I deal with what are called *primitive* mythologies, or with Oriental mythologies, I see that nature is regarded as a manifestation of something that's basically divine and marvelous and miraculous, and, by putting yourself in accord with nature, you participate in that glory. But when I turn to our Western mythologies—as they exist in our spiritual traditions—I find a totally different point of view. And I've been wondering, "How did this happen? Where does this come from?"

Well, the first stage in the transformation comes from a system of religions that appears around the first millennium BC in the Near East—not the Far East, but the Near East. Its principal representative, outside of the Judaic-Christian line, is Zoroastrianism. In Zoroastrianism, it is believed that a good creator created a good world and a bad counter-creator threw evil into it. So we have a dual creation—good and evil, light and darkness, virtue and vice, truth and hypocrisy, and so on. We have this also in our biblical story of the Fall in the Garden of Eden. There is a conflict between a good and an evil force, and we are invited to make the decision to align ourselves with the good. Now, we are not asked to put ourselves in accord with a split nature like that; rather we are asked to correct it! The world that we're living in today is also a combination of this duality. This accounts for the tremendous accent on action in our culture. That's one of the big, big problems.

The second problem is that the origin of this tradition is Semitic. The Semitic people come from the desert, and one of the characteristics of the Semitic religions—whether it's Babylonian or Acadian, Hebrew or Assyrian—is that the main deity is not a personification of the powers of nature, but of the principles and ethics and history of that society.

When you have a nature religion—and, by the way, this is a derogatory term that

refs to all the religions of the world except this cluster I am talking about—you
can say, for example, "The deity whom
you call Indra, we call Zeus." When Caesar went into Gaul in the sixth book of his
Gallic Wars, he describes the religions of
the Celtic people of Gaul, but he uses the
Latin names for the deities. This is called
syncretism. Similarly, when Alexander the
Great went into India, his officers immediately recognized the relationship of the Indian deities to their own. They identified
Krishna with Heracles, and so forth. But,
when your principal deity is the deity of
your tribe, this can't be done. When your
main deity is your tribal deity, you cannot
say, "He whom you call Ashur, we call
Yahweh." Rather you get a basic exclusivism not only from nature but also from
your neighbors. There's a contention
against the neighbors who are nature religion worshipers, who are worshiping

wrong gods, false gods, and all that kind of thing. And this exclusivism is built right into us because it is fundamental to the Judaic-Christian tradition.

A third force is that our mainstream religions in the West are scriptural and were formulated a little over two thousand years ago in another place. Therefore, we have been unable to sanctify our land. Our land doesn't speak to us of the divine. Divine land is only over there in the Middle East. We make pilgrimages to the Holy Land, or people go there to claim it from another people and make it their own again. This is a historical misinterpretation of spiritual symbols. The Holy Land isn't in some other place. It's right in here — right inside each of us!

You've spent years writing about gods. Most people today would say the gods are dead. Are they alive and if they're alive where are they?

Oh, this business of the gods. . . . You see, in our religious training we're not put in a position to understand what gods are in other traditions.

The gods are personifications of the energies that inform life—the very energies that are building the trees and moving the animals and whipping up the waves on the ocean. The very energies that are in your body are personified by the gods. They're alive and well in everybody's life.

Most traditions realize this—that deities are personifications, not facts. They are metaphors. They're not references to anything that you can put your finger on, or your eye on. They are metaphors transparent to transcendence. But in our religious training we are not put in a position to understand how the gods are seen in other religious traditions so we have lost this language of the spirit. We do not recognize the gods.

Now, a deity that is not recognized and revered and allowed to play into our conscious life becomes an idol. It closes itself and is no longer transparent to transcendence. The energy gets blocked and becomes what we call a devil. The deity goes into reverse and becomes a negative power, a threatening power. When we forget the deities, we build a life on a program run by the head. The energies coming from the body are ignored and become threatening to the values, the head values, which we have chosen to live for. It's as easy as that.

What happened in our tradition—and it is quite peculiar to this tradition, which is biblically based—is that the god was regarded as a fact. Instead of being a personification of energies that are antecedent to his personification, he was understood to be the source of the energies. This means that the god doesn't refer past himself. He is closed. He says, "This is it. I'm a jealous god. There is no other god but me." And then we're in trouble.

Why?

We're in trouble because we don't recognize that the god's energies are our *own* energies. We don't understand that the energies personified in the god are the very energies of our own lives. We don't realize that the gods are not out there somewhere. They live in us all. They are the energies of life itself.

This is the great realization of the Upanishads as early as the tenth or ninth century BC — "You are it." The mystery that you're looking for and you think is somewhere external to yourself is not out there at all. It's what you are. You don't have to go anywhere to find god, and you don't have to go anywhere to find the

Promised Land. It's here, inside every human being. It's where you are. It's what you are.

There is a wonderful little book by John Neihardt, *Black Elk Speaks.* Black Elk was a Sioux keeper of the sacred pipe, a great shaman. In his boyhood he had a vision. Shamanic visions often come in early life and are prophetic of the whole life dynamic that the unconscious life knows about — the unconscious knows what your possibilities are and will tell you in your dreams. Black Elk said, "At one moment in my dream I saw myself in the central mountain of the world, and the central mountain of the world was Harney Peak in South Dakota." And then he added immediately, "But the central mountain is everywhere." Now there's a man who knows the difference between the cult and its reference.

In order to bring the people together,

in order to hold your mind to something, you have to have a metaphor that points past itself. For Black Elk, Harney Peak is a metaphor that points past itself and represents energies personified in our life. But does Jerusalem point past itself? Does Rome point past itself? No, they don't! They are closed, fixed in time and space.

How has this come about in our culture?

Well, there are only two ways to misunderstand a myth and our civilization has managed to do both. One is to think that the myth refers to a geographical or historical fact—Jesus rose from the dead, Moses got the law at the top of the mountain, that sort of thing. The other is to think that the myth refers to a supernatural fact, or to an actual event that's going to happen in the future—the resurrection of Jesus, or the second coming. Our whole religious tradition is based upon these two misunderstandings. One, the misunderstanding of myth as reference to historical facts; the other, misunderstanding myth as reference to spiritual facts either of something that is somewhere invisible, or something that is going to happen sometime in the future. It's a terrible tragedy. These misunderstandings of our myth have caused us to lose the vocabulary of the spirit.

When the Oriental gurus come over here, they say, "What does it matter if someone rose from the dead two thousand years ago? Are you rising from the dead today? Are you pulling your spiritual, your human consciousness out of your animal base and letting the animal base become spiritualized in your life experience?" They're right. That's what's important. And that's what the myths are about.

2 · SYMBOLS

I HAD A VERY interesting, amusing experience about three weeks ago. I was having lunch with a young woman who was from Israel. She had just come from Guatemala, where she had paid a visit to the ruins down there—very exciting. She'd had a wonderful time. But in the little Guatemalan city of Antigua, the chambermaid had asked her, "Where are you from?"

"Oh," she said, "I'm from Jerusalem."

"What!" said the chambermaid. "You are from the sky?"

Now, this is a wrong interpretation of the symbol of the Promised Land—that it's somewhere in the spiritual sky. The other wrong interpretation is that it's a piece of geography somewhere on this planet. The Christian tradition has one mistake; the Hebrew tradition has the other. And the other people who seem to be bringing the message of where the Promised Land really is are the gurus who are coming over here and running away with all the chickens. Anyone who wants to find where his spiritual life is located need not go and hear, "It's in the sky," or "Get yourself a gun and go to Israel." It's right here inside each and every one of us.

Now, this word *symbol* as I've been using it has a specific reference. I mean it's optional how you define words like that. Jung distinguishes between the *symbol* and the *sign.* A sign is a reference to something that is known or knowable in a perfectly rational way. For instance, you come along a road to a sign that says, "To Boston," the sign "stands for" a knowable, physical place. But a symbol, a mythic symbol, does not refer to something which is known or knowable in that rational way. It refers to a spiritual power that is operative in life and is known only through its effects.

The other term that often comes up with *sign* and *symbol* is *allegory*. In poetry and literature, an allegory is a way of talking about something that's already known—talking about it in an interesting way through images. For instance, the twelfth-century allegory of the *Romance of the Rose* is an allegory of love, and every element in that story represents some emotional relationship to the experience of moving into a love affair. That's an allegory.

But take the symbol of the Virgin Birth. It is not a sign. It is not an allegorical reference. It is not a reference to an historical fact. It's a reference to a spiritual event, and if it's interpreted as referring to a historical event, it is misread. The symbol of the Promised Land, for instance, has nothing to do with a geographical area that has to be conquered and maintained by military might. It is a reference to a place, or what might be called an attitude toward a place, in the human heart. In this place, the heart is a still point from which the four rivers flow. That's the Promised Land. It's to be found in oneself spiritually and realized in life. It's a potentiality, not a fact. There's a big difference there.

One of the things that's happened in our Western religions is that many of the symbols have been misinterpreted as signs, and our whole mythology is read as a pseudo-history which never took place historically. And that's why, when people realize that it couldn't have taken place, they lose their faith and their religion, and then they're without the vocabulary of the communication between the transcendent and the rationality of a living human being. That's what I see around us all the time.

Does the god Janus, with his two faces looking in opposite directions, relate to what you are saying?

We have the indication of the meaning of the god Janus in the name January, the first month of the year, which starts the New Year. This is the figure of the New Year looking in the two directions—a pair of opposites.

Now, one of the essential elementary ideas that runs through all truly mythological systems is that of the pair of opposites. This refers to the fact that in space and time we experience life as opposites. In the Janus figure, the two opposites are actually one—one figure looking in the two directions. This points to the way we experience time. It's in the past, and it's in the future, but the *now* runs down the middle. So, when we have a two-faced figure like Janus, the point we are supposed to concentrate on is the middle. The two faces are the two aspects which we experience in our temporal life. For example, Adam and Eve are simply the two aspects of one being. They were thrown out of the Garden of Eden when they knew the difference between good and evil. At that point, they also knew the difference between male and female. They also knew the difference between man and God. So they were out! And the only way to get back in is to get to the middle again. Heraclitus tells us, "For God all things are good and right but for men some things are good and some things are evil." That's the purely temporal aspect of where we split.

Now, a very important dual figure of this kind is the *androgyne,* the male/female who are one. This is the prime symbol of the realization of opposites. Marriage is an occasion for coming to an experience that transcends your own personal incarnation of one aspect, and, through the relationship in marriage, you may experience an identity with that other you, that is, experience your participation in the androgyne motif.

One after another, these dual aspects can be rendered in myths. Primitive mythologies of hunting people express the human being and animals as one—semi-human, semi-animal figures. Dancing shamans who look like men but also have animal features appear in the caves in southern France. They were painted perhaps thirty thousand years ago. Also, in the myths of American Indians or of the hunting people of Africa, we have these dual images pointing to the middle between the two opposites. Of course, to interpret the motif you must find out what the two sides represent. With respect to the god Janus, since he is associated with January, the image tells us the New Year is the old way coming back—two faces but looking in opposite directions. The *now* is the middle where they join. The *now* runs along as a constant.

Would you interpret the symbolism of the Virgin Birth?

The Virgin Birth—we know what its meaning is. It occurs in most of the mythologies of the world—American Indian mythologies, Oriental mythologies, all over the place. The references to these births in the heart of the human animal is to the realization that there are aims in life other than those of the maintenance and reproduction of our animal species. It's also called the Second Birth. The birth of the spiritual as opposed to simply the natural life. The whole function of mythological and ritual instruction is to transform the person who lives for animal ends into one who lives for cultural and spiritual ends. The individual who teaches these aims, these aspects of life—who really teaches them—is one who has experienced them. He himself has experienced the Second Birth. He has gone through the Virgin Birth and been born again. You can see that to translate that back into a biological birth, as Christianity has done, is to completely miss the message.

In the Hindu Kundalini system, which describes the spiritual stages of development of the psyche, there are three chakras, or, as they are called, *wheels* or *lotuses,* located in the pelvic area. These have to do with the animal aims of generating new life, of clinging to life, and of conquering and mastering the world around you. Then, at the level of the heart, the level of the Virgin Birth, there's a transformation. Now, this symbolism is beautiful. On the lowest chakra, the symbol for the physical generation of biological life is the natural one of the male and female organs in conjunction. Also, at the level of the heart, we have the same symbol again of the male and female organs in union, but here it is gold and symbolizes the generation of a spiritual entity—the Virgin Birth. Until that comes, you have only a human animal not a human being. That is what the Virgin Birth is about.

The Virgin Birth is always a miraculous birth. The Buddha, for example, was born from his mother's side, from exactly the level of that heart chakra. Of course, he wasn't physically born that way at all but that is symbolic of his life. The biography of a spiritual teacher is not an account of historical facts, like Carl Sandburg's biography of Lincoln. It is a symbol of the spiritual biography of that man, and all of the elements of the biography are symbolic. Just through reading them properly you learn the message.

For example, take the story of the three temptations of Christ. First, he goes to John the Baptist, one of the greatest teachers of the time. Then he goes past him, past his teacher, into the desert to have his own experience. The first temptation in the desert is the economic one, "Command that these stones be made bread." He rejects this, "Man lives by every word out of the mouth of God." Next is the political one, "Bow down before me and you can rule the world." (I don't know how many politicians realize the impact of that.) Jesus also rejects the devil there. Having rejected the economic and political aims of life, he could have felt spiritually inflated, so the myth goes on to a third temptation in which the devil takes Jesus

to the top of Herod's temple and says,
"Oh, you are so spiritual. Just cast yourself
down." To understand this image you have
only to go to many ashrams where you
will find people up on the top of the temple. They're so spiritualized they are quite
certain that they could cast themselves
down and God wouldn't allow the stones
to bruise their heel. But Jesus said, "Now,
look, thou shall not tempt the Lord thy
God. I am still body and must realize the
spiritual in the living body." This is the
great teaching of all the greatest teachers—not to disengage yourself from natural life and law, but, at the same time, not
to become bound to the world of sensory
fact.

Now, the Hindus really have these
truths in beautiful images. There's the notion of bringing the energies of the psyche
up from the ground base, right up the
spine to the crown of the head through a

channel known as the *sushumna*. On either side of this channel run two nerves: one has to do with the material, geographical, historical interpretation of the symbols, the other has to do with the purely spiritual interpretation of the symbols. Our traditions tend to these two types of interpretation rather than focusing on the middle. This is unfortunate, for it's the middle that says the experience is in you, it's right in here. The Virgin Birth is the birth in you and the Promised Land is a land that you're to find in yourself.

How do you account for the number of people in our Western society who believe in a fundamentalist type of religion which holds to a firm concretization of the Christian myth?

Well, good old four-square religion is based on a cosmology, or rather an idea of the cosmos, that dates from 2000 BC, and these people know damn well that it's a lot of nonsense. This contributes to the violence of their message—trying to convince themselves that it's true by making other people say it's true. This is one of the great, what might be called psychological, forces inspiring missions. What's basic to this whole thing is not simply that "god is a fact," but that your whole ethnic inheritance of the name and characterization of god is a fact, rather than simply a symbol referring to something transcendent. The psyche damn well knows that this is not true. This is what's called idolatry—mistaking the symbol for the reference. And this is the mistake of what might be called the fundamentalist position with respect to biblical symbols. They say, "God is a fact. He does love the Jews more than anybody else." Who could believe this bit of nonsense? One knows unconsciously it's not true, and this unconscious knowledge moves them to try to convince everybody else that it is true so as to confirm themselves in their own nonsense. Then they see idolatry everywhere other than right in their own tradition, where it really is. They cannot see that these other traditions are not idolatrous, cannot be idolatrous, because their gods are symbols, not facts.

This is the history of the Western conquest of the planet, and now what's got to happen, unless we're going to blow this thing to smithereens, is the Western recognition that other people had it before we got to it, namely, that gods are personifications of powers that are in you and in the universe and not simply out there or up there. This is what I see as the problem of the Western religiosity and mentality in relation to the modern world.

How do you interpret the symbol of the Fall?

The Fall in the Hebrew tradition, which we have inherited, is in the same context basically as the Zoroastrian tradition. It is a recognition that life in time is not life in eternity. Now to interpret this as a fall you must see nature as a mixture of good and evil. You must separate out the good and favor it against the evil. Of course, this interpretation separates us from nature and I believe it underlies a good deal of the violence of Western progressivism.

What the Fall represents is indicated in the serpent. The serpent in most traditions represents the power of life to throw off death, the energy of life in the field of time. When it becomes negative, life is condemned. Humans do not yield to the serpent. This has been our traditional way of interpreting this symbol, and I think it's pathological. I really do. I don't think there's any way to justify it.

You don't see it then as a fall but exactly the opposite.

I don't see being born as a fall. I see it as a triumph, a joyful participation. Christ voluntarily moving to the cross. That's the way to talk about life, not as, "Oh dear, look what happened to me, I got born." I remember I had that experience once when I was studying deeply with a yogi. It suddenly dawned on me that this was a man who said when he came into this world, "Oh, no! I'm going back. I can't take this." He wanted out of life.

What effect do you think these Eastern religions coming into our Western culture are having?

I think they are having a very good effect. I think they are helping even the high clergy to translate historically interpreted

symbols into spiritual symbols. I was lecturing out at a very strongly Catholic sem-
inary, I won't say where, and I found that
a number of the priests there were actually
studying Zen, which has to do with the
recognition of Buddha consciousness as
being not outside the individual, but right
inside. They teach that all the symbolic
talk is only to help you come to that realization, and, if it's not helping you, then
throw it away, just point inside and say,
"It's here." That's the sense of the saying,
"If you see the Buddha coming along the
road, kill him." He's not out there. He's
in here. If you concretize your symbol and
see the answer to everything in one external form, you have become an idolater, so
kill it.

*Many people would disagree with you on the
basis of what they say the Bible says.*

Ahhh, don't tell me—the Bible is a compendium of all the mistakes that have ever been made in the translation of symbolic forms into historical. It's a total compendium. You see, that's popular. That's easy. In *Finnegans Wake* James Joyce uses the name Hume the Cheapener as one of the names for his hero. I remember my friend Henry Morton Robinson, with whom I worked on *The Skeleton Key,* saying that "the cheapener" seemed to be the lowest thing you could say about any man. Well, that's what I think a lot of our popular religion has done. It has cheapened the high spiritual symbols into chauvinistic advertisements of our own culture and its superiority to others.

Joe, would you call yourself a Christian?

No.

Well then, how do you define yourself in terms of a religion?

I don't.

Would you say you're not a Christian?

I wouldn't say that either.

Those terms don't mean anything to you?

Well, they don't apply to my condition. I'm not a fish either. I was once, perhaps. I know I was a Christian. Similarly with my scholarship, I can't say what it is I'm studying. I don't know. One of the problems, of course, in academic life is that you get into a box and study only one narrow field, like some medical men now who study only the right wrist or something like that. They know what's necessary there but they can't treat the left wrist. I speak of this from experience. My wife, Jean, broke her wrist and the doctor who fixed it up did a marvelous job. Five years later when she was having problems again with the wrist, he said, "Oh, I'm not working on the wrist now. I'm working on the back." We get the same specialization in the academic world as well. Anyone who studies two totally different departments of life is called a "generalist" and that's a term of derogation. And I would say that we tend to over specialization in our religious thinking as well.

And how do you foresee the future?

I don't. I mean there are so many factors pushing in. When I was a boy in college, who would have thought of the things that are now operating in the world? The computer for example. What's that doing to amplify our consciousness? Or rocket propulsion, which has opened space in a way that is absolutely incredible, and jet propulsion, airplanes that move you from here to Japan in less than twenty-four hours, bringing the world together in an unprecedented way. Today, we see people in our classrooms whom we would never have known existed in the world fifty years ago, and they would have had no knowledge of our culture either. The people of the world are just beginning to come together. It's a fantastic period!

Now, with respect to mythology, the same old motifs are going to be there. They're going to *have* to be there. They're the motifs of human life. But they're going to have to be related to a new social consciousness — not one of the tribe, not even of the planet. And until that happens, what might be called the new and appropriate mythology for a global consciousness will not have taken place.

Just think, for instance, of that picture of the earth taken from the moon. There you don't see the old tribal consciousness, or a planetary consciousness. In that picture of the earth there is something much bigger, and, when the mythological motifs are related to social consciousness, it will feel something like looking at the earth from the moon.

People today are still pulling back into their in-group commitments all over the place. It's as though there were a reluctance to make the jump that has to be made of recognizing in one's fellow man a totally different race, and skin color, and religion. The result is that people link themselves with one group against another group, rather than adopting an attitude, "I can play ball on my team but that doesn't turn me against the other team."

To play the role of history and, at the same time, participate in the undifferentiated view is the problem of myth. It's caught in that wonderful little image from the Vedas that I love to refer to of the two birds on the tree of life. One eats the fruit and the other, not eating, watches. It says, "If you're going to act, you're eating the fruit. You're killing." That's what life is.

Look at the animals or the birds! All they're doing is killing other things and eating them—the grass or other animals or whatnot. But there is another of us who watches. In a tennis match you're trying to beat the guy on the other side of the net but there is also the umpire's position. In sports this is known as good sportsmanship. There is an old Eskimo saying, "To win a dogsled race is great; to lose, that's all right too." That kind of double optic, double view, is what myth asks you to take. We must play our historical role, but that is only our historical role. In life, we put on the mask of a certain race, a certain

time, a certain group of ethical commitments, and so forth, and we stand for
those, but we also know that what we are
is only one half of something that the
other fellow represents on the other side.

That's the only way of aristocratic bat-
tle, the knightly conflict. There was a relationship of honor between knights. Those
men did not despise each other. If they
did, they wouldn't use their swords; that
would be an insult to the sword. We don't
have this sense of knightly conflict anymore. Since Napoleon's time, the mythology of our enemy as the demon and ourselves as bright radiant heroes has been
built up. That's a mythology all right, only
it's concretized. There is no middle.

*Don't you think that interpreting mythology
in this way can be destructive? Are you not
smashing down people's religious beliefs?*

Well, I think exactly the opposite. Out of my own experience teaching comparative mythology for thirty-eight years in a college, what happened was that when the students learned how to read symbols, they looked back at the symbols of their own religion and knew what they were saying. Instead of knocking it out, it reconfirmed it and linked it to their own lives. That was the way it struck me, and I know in my own case, I now think I understand the symbology of the Christian religion, which I dropped fifty-odd years ago because it wasn't making sense. It was untrue. Couldn't have been true. Well, it's damn true in the way of symbolic truth and I know it. That doesn't mean I have to go to church and listen to some priest or minister who doesn't know what he's talking about tell me to contribute to the coal fund. It's a different thing. A lot of people think that you have to go to church to be religious. This is a purely Western idea.

You said that a symbol is talking to you whether you understand it or not. Would you clarify that?

A symbol is talking to you and, whether the head knows it or not, the heart knows it. And the heart also knows when you're being misinformed as to the symbol's meaning. There comes a dissonance. For example, an amusing thing happens when a patriarchal religion takes over matriarchal symbols—the male tries to put himself in the female's position. Now, who wants Abraham's bosom? The image doesn't give me much comfort. You see, you can't do it. You simply can't kick mother out of the house and put daddy in her place, and the psyche knows it.

3 · GODDESSES

WITH PEOPLE NOW it's becoming quite fashionable to realize that God is female as well as male. In Genesis 1, God creates Adam and Eve in his own image—"male and female created he them." And so the God idea, if you're going to make any sense of it whatsoever, has to be transcendent of this sexual polarity—God is beyond polarities; God is even beyond the polarity of being and nonbeing. For instance, think of the question, "Do you believe in God?" Well, I can't answer that. I don't know an answer because the question makes no sense. You see, *God* is a metaphor for something transcendent of the metaphor itself.

So now people are beginning to get excited about the god *and* the goddess, and since the only goddess anyone seems to know anything about is the mother goddess, they're all interested in the mother. But all you have to do is read the *Odyssey* to know that the goddess can appear in other aspects.

I will talk now from the standpoint of the male in relation to the female image. First, the goddess as mother. You are still a child. You have to break from the mother's house, move into adulthood, and then one of the other aspects of the goddess will appear. Who are they? Well, I can't speak for the Chinese and Tibetans but I can speak for the Europeans from the time of the *Odyssey*. Odysseus met them. They were three nymphs. They were Circe, Calypso, and Nausicaa.

Circe is the seductress, the temptress, the one who leads us into the world of sin. That's to say, sin as an experience of life outside of the social roles, outside of the social norms. Here we see the woman as initiator, a conduit between the particular, local experience and the larger, universal experience. What our ethically oriented religion doesn't seem to realize is that the metaphysical and the transcendent go beyond the local ethical system. So it's a surprise that Circe is actually the initiator of Odysseus. Circe, the pig woman, turns men into swine and then, when they're turned back into men, they're handsomer and wiser than before. She introduced Odysseus to the mysteries of the underworld, the world of the biological ground out of which all life comes forth. And what does he meet in the underworld? He meets a lot of spooks, but he also meets Tiresias, that sage who had been a woman as well as a man and represents the thing that is the biological ground—the androgyne motif. He understands that the male is not superior to the female as the male was in the *Iliad,* where woman was simply property or booty. After this experience, Odysseus sees woman as the counter player, the other side of this dual being, the androgyne. Then he comes back to Circe and she says to him, "Now that you've learned that lesson, you can go to the island of my father, the God of the Sun," who represents total consciousness. So she introduces him first to the biological ground, that dark abyss out of which our life comes, and then to the totally luminous consciousness, which we can also experience. Now, these two are the same. They're two aspects of the same.

The second role is that of Calypso, the wife, who is the one who integrates this realization with the living of a harmonious and productive life. She is the one who restores the man who's been shattered by the temptress and the seductress initiator. She puts him back together again into life.

Woman as temptress, woman as wife, and now, woman as daughter—the little Nausicaa, the virgin goddess, the virgin nymph—the lovely charm of life. Because the female is the image of life and the male is the image of achievement, the woman's body is the basic body. It's the body out of which life comes. The male's body is a body to defend that basic body, to set up a field within which it can function and bring forth. When women don't realize that anymore then they've lost their womanhood to the male propaganda that worldly or social achievement is something that's important. Such achievement is meaningless when it does not honor the life impulse. It's the ladder against the wrong wall.

Now, these three goddesses—three nymphs—Circe, Calypso, and Nausicaa,

correspond exactly to the three great goddesses. Circe, the seductress, corresponds
to Aphrodite, the goddess of lust representing the dynamic of the erotic powers.
Calypso, the wife, is the counterpart of the
great goddess Hera, the consort of Zeus,
who represents the mature energy principle, represented in a man's life as gover-
nor, a man in control of life, a man of authority. And Nausicaa is the counterpart
of Athena. She's a patron saint of heroes —
she supports them — but she's also a
hero-worshiper.

It's interesting that these three goddesses are exactly the three that in the
Judgement of Paris stood before, what we
used to call in my boyhood, "a lounge liz-
ard" — a guy who judges women as though
it were a beauty contest. Jane Harrison,
a classical scholar of the last generation,
pointed out that this was a put-down of
the female power, that the male power had

put down the three main goddesses of the classical pre-Homeric pantheon: Aphrodite, the goddess of love who informs the whole universe; Hera, the consort of Zeus who represents power and energy functioning in the field of time; and Athena, the patron goddess of heroic deeds. Having put them down, you are left quite simply with two ideas of women—property and booty, which is the attitude the warrior holds toward woman. In the *Iliad* that is the way woman appears. When Agamemnon and Achilles come to deal with the captured Trojan girl, Briseis, the question is, "Who gets the blonde?" This is no way to relate to the female in a mature, male/female, androgyne relationship. So it's Circe who introduces Odysseus to the recovery from that male put-down and to getting a good domestic relationship to the female power. As he's returning from ten years of warrior life, where women are booty, to his domestic life, the gods see to it that he gets these initiations of three females—the same three that were put down.

Now, if people don't have a notion of who they are when they're in a certain life relationship to the opposite sex, they may have no image to give meaning to what is happening to them and not know how to proceed. Say, for example, that the person receiving the impact of a love, being smitten by a love—and, you know, that kind of thing does happen, and it's a calamity if you go through life without ever having had it happen—say this person has a very elementary idea of relationship, so is forced to ask questions like "How do I relate this love to my actual social condition? To my actual age? To the actual role that I'm playing?" If the person has only one image of relationship, namely, jumping into bed, then there will be great difficulties handling the power of love. There are many ways of relating this tremendous experience of the male/female identity both in transcendence and to the actualities of a life, and that's what the myth helps us to see. I hear often from so many young people, "Oh, we had a love affair, but now we're friends." So they have two images of relationship: one is friendship, and the other is lust. That's not enough. There are plenty of ways to relate, and the myths give these clues.

There is a prayer from the twelfth or thirteenth century which indicates two different mythological possibilities. "O Lord, who taught Mary to conceive without sinning, teach me to sin without conceiving." Here are two totally different mythologies in collision with each other. The one, of delight in a life which is regarded as being sinful; the other, as the zeal to bring forth the world's savior. Well, when you're caught between those with no bridge, you're in a pretty bad spot, I think.

Would you distinguish Aphrodite from the principle of unrelated sexuality, of promiscuity, or is that the energy she personifies?

Aphrodite is no whore really. She is not a prostitute. A prostitute is a kind of spin-off, you might say, from Aphrodite, in which she's moved into the realm of commerce. As soon as you get into the realm of commerce, you've lost touch. This is true in the arts too, and is the problem of the commercial artist. "What can I do to make money from my art?" not, "How's my art enabling me to flower?" This is an important problem.

What distinguishes Aphrodite from promiscuity?

The fact that Aphrodite represents a power that has nothing to do with commercial or social advantage; she is simply the impact of Eros on one.

One of the great moments of the twelfth and thirteenth centuries was the introduction of courtly love in the troubadour tradition. Until then, marriage had always been looked at as a social business. The couple being married often had never even seen each other. This still goes on in the Orient and in many parts of the world to this day—I was interested to see in New Delhi that the daily newspapers carried columns of advertisements for wives put in by families or by marriage brokers. The requirements had nothing to do with the meeting of the eyes of two individuals, and in that sense the erotic relationship had nothing to do with the individual experience of Eros. It was impersonal, and, in that context, without recognition of the individual experience. Now, in religious discussions of Eros, there were, and still are, two parts, both of which are impersonal. First is lust, which I define as a purely biological zeal of the organs for each other, and the other is *agape* or spiritual love—love thy neighbor as thyself. Both are impersonal. Well, it's in the twelfth century, with the troubadours, that a new idea of *amour,* love, emerges. *Amour* is seen as personal and as a primary principle in the shaping of an aristocratic society.

The troubadours had many debates as to what the definition of love would be. One of the most interesting and precise debates states that the eyes are the scouts for the heart, and the eyes go forth to find an image to recommend to the heart. When the image is found and recommended, if the heart is a gentle heart— that is to say, a heart that is capable of love and not simply of lust — then love is born. If, on the other hand, it is not a gentle heart, then all you have is lust — the pig heart. You don't have love. And the problem of the woman in the twelfth and thirteenth century courtly tradition was to guarantee to herself that the address of the man challenging her love was not of lust but of a gentle heart. This idea of a gentle heart or, in another sense, the noble heart, is a basic one to twelfth and thirteenth century romance and is a very important thing. It represents a stage, you might say, of psychological transformation.

Why is it so important?

It's important because it brings into the field of actual cultural traditions and ideals a principle that is of individual, and not simply general, biological significance. The whole meaning of the Grail tradition has to do with the problem of a person living an authentic life out of the spontaneity of his heart when that heart is a noble heart whose spontaneity is based on compassion rather than possession and conquest. In the Grail tradition, the individual was conscious of facing the wasteland, a land of people who do simply what they are supposed to do, or what is thought by the society well to do—people professing beliefs because they have to, holding jobs that they've inherited, not earned, and so forth—a group of zombies, you might say. That's what the story of Perceval represents in the Grail romances—the principle of compassion with suffering, in which you recognize your essential transpersonal identity with the very life that's there facing you. That's what the Grail legend is all about.

In discussing the goddesses in mythology, we touched on the mother only very briefly. Could we talk more fully about what she represents?

Well, the mother in mythology is a magnificent power, which the culture never gets away from. The culture is always dependent on her, particularly an agricultural culture. She is the one who has to supply the rebirths, the new generations coming through. The individual's task is to break out of that, to leave mother behind, and become the one who guides and helps the culture.

Now, this is a point that for me is very important. We're getting too much culture stuff now and not enough individual resilience, individual courage, and individual action. Our religions are primarily ethical religions, which stem from all this bargaining thing of sin and atonement. There is a wonderful passage of Ramakrishna, a wonderful Indian saint of the nineteenth century. Someone had given him a Bible to read and he said, "I've been reading the Bible and all I find is sin, sin, sin, sin. If

you think you're a sinner, you're a sinner."
Well, I can certainly remember as a kid, I
was a sinner. Every Saturday, I went over
the sins I committed that week. And the
problem with that approach is simply that,
if you meditate on your past sins long
enough, you can get lost in your sins and
not know what your virtues are. Why not
meditate on the virtues? Foster the virtues
and let the sins fall off. Find the virtues.
Affirm life! Instead of criticizing it, affirm
life!

*What are some great mythic images of the
mother?*

The images of the mother? My God,
there's a virtual glorious art display of this
wonderful figure! There's a very interesting geographical polarity, though. East of
Suez, you won't see many Madonnas.
You'll see the mother goddess as a fosterer

of children, but they're not necessarily her children. There are few nursing Madonna forms. They are very, very rare and usually of Western influence. It's in the West where you have the nursing Madonna, and that image starts very early in Mesopotamia. Here we have the nursing mother, which represents that sustainer of life, and then, of course, it comes over in the Madonna image of the Christian tradition. But look at the Madonnas.

When you look at the Byzantine Madonnas you don't see the nursing mother very much. What you do see is the mother sitting there as the throne, and the little king of the world sitting on her lap—just as Pharaoh sits on the throne, and the throne is the goddess Isis. She is the world support, and he is an agent of her will. And that's what the male is, an agent of the female will. He sits on her lap, and she, the female, is the life power.

Are you suggesting that a man should be dominated by a woman?

No, not dominated by the woman. The power that the man is fostering is primarily represented in the woman more than in himself. He is the fosterer. She is the symbol of the power. In the myths, the male is the agent of the will that the woman represents—not her personal will.

With the first menstruation, a girl is overcome by nature. It's not her will. And so she represents life, you see, and the male in relation to the female is also an agent, an executive of the same life. Each has a role in relation to it. She carries it; he supports her and protects her. I'm speaking from the standpoint of the old biological ground, which these religions represent. And so in a marriage, for instance, if a man thinks, "Oh, I'm just obeying my wife," he's got it wrong. It's nothing of the kind. She knows a little more than he does about what life is, because it's done more to her, and from her he can learn.

What other energies does the mother personify in mythology?

Well, when you think of the mother from a mythological point of view, there are perhaps three or four basic images. The first is Mother Earth, out of which all life springs. We'll call this the vegetable world.

The second is Mother Universe, which is a development out of Mother Earth. In Egypt, for example, the goddess Nut is the sky. Now, we usually think of mother as the earth, but here you have the mother as the sky itself, mother as the totality of the enclosing world within which we live, so that we're all, as it were, within the mother womb.

Now, in Indian philosophy and mythology, the mother is called *Maya* — the principle that measures out. This isn't just a personal mother. This isn't just the earth. This is the whole mystery of the mind. All the forms of life are experienced by our mind. We don't know what they are. We don't know what it is. Everything we experience is in the field of time and space, and in the field of time and space all things are broken up into separate things, so we may say that what we experience is separate within the womb of the mother. The mother then is time, and space, and causality.

As well, when we think about the things that we experience, we can think only in terms of categories, which are also the mother. So the image of the mother goes from the simple Earth Mother to the Cosmic Mother, to the concept of the mother of all our concepts, and all our thoughts.

We are bounded by this body and its limitations, and that is our mother field.

Also, we have another mother image, which occurs after the rise of cities. Here you see goddesses with a crown on their heads, which represents the walls of the city. The walled city is our mother, the mother of our civilization, the mother of our life. So the culture is also our mother.

Now, I was brought up a little Catholic boy and we had images of the Virgin Mother and the Madonna all around the house, and I learned to experience my mother, my personal mother, as my local representative of the principle of motherhood represented in the image of the Virgin. It's a beautiful thing to experience the loveliness of your own mother as a manifestation for you of the loveliness of a whole principle that's in the world, that's in the universe. And this is one of the sweet things in being brought up in the tradition, like the Roman Catholic, where the goddess takes the form of Mary, the mother of God—nobody could ask for a bigger assignment. The sense here is that the image of God is already an image, whereas the transcendent is beyond imitation. So the image of God and the name of God are in the field of the mother, which gives all names and forms. All of this comes to you in your mother as representative of this mother principle. She's both a giver and a disciplinarian. But in Catholicism, as in other Christian religions, there is a problem. The goddess is split in two. You have the beneficient Madonna all right, but you also have the hell hag, the witch—the negative.

In the East, these two are put together in the wonderful goddess Kali. The word *kali* means *black time,* that time out of which all things come and into which all things return. Seen in these two aspects, one is the giver and one is the taker of life. She is represented with four hands. One right hand says, "Don't be afraid." The other right hand offers you a bowl of rice. One left hand carries a sword, and in the other she holds a head which she has severed. This is the goddess representing the totality of the life dynamic. Again in the Orient, the word for energy, *shakti,* is female. Energy is the female principle. The female is the awakener of energies. The male, for example, is at peace with himself, but when a shining, twinkling female invitation goes by, he is immediately activated. She is the activator and then when the male is activated, she's surprised. She is the activator and then is acted upon. Those are her two aspects.

Do institutions and corporations often act as mothers?

When you fly to protection, or when you don't have to take care of yourself but are taken care of, then you're in the mother's arms, so, in a certain sense, the firm or company that you're working for is the mother. Particularly in the way it works in Japan. When a person passes his exams in a certain university at a certain level, he gets a position in a big firm that protects him for life. He's gone, as it were, back into the mother. Then, when he loses his job, it's a terrible thing, particularly in a welfare state, where the state is the mother incarnate. I mean you don't even have to think! The less you do, the more it does for you. It's one sure way to infantilism. The whole population turns into children. And then, if somebody comes along and cuts the dole, you hear, "You can't do this! I'm out on my own! This is terrible!" Well, you know, every squirrel knows how to take care of itself. The welfare state is the mother, all right, in her all-absorbing power—"Won't you come to me darling? I'll take care of you. Kiss mama!"

4 · INITIATIONS

I 'M A SCHOLAR. I read. I remember my friend Alan Watts once asked me, "Joe, what is your yoga?" And I said, "My yoga is underlining sentences." Old Will Rogers used to say, "All I know is what I read in the newspapers." Well, all I know is what I read in books—with a little bit more added.

The rituals of initiation of young men in some of the very simple societies are extremely interesting. The boys are brought up to be in fear of the masks, which the men wear in their rituals. The masks are the gods. They are the personifications of the powers that structure the society. When the boy gets to be more than his mother can handle, the men come

in with their masks, or whatever their cos-
tume is, and grab the kid. He thinks he's
been taken by the gods. He is taken out to
the men's grounds and, among other
things, he's beaten up.

In New Guinea, there's a wonderful,
wonderful event where the poor kid has
to stand up to fight a man with a mask.
They tell him that he's fighting a god. The
man lets the kid win and then takes the
mask off and puts it on the boy. Now, it's
important that the mask is in no way de-
feated. Rather, putting the mask on the
boy means, "Now you're a man. You've
broken past the image as face and understand the image as metaphor, and you are
to represent what the metaphor stands
for." The mask represents the power that
is shaping the society and is shaping the
boy. After the mask is put on him, he is a
representative of that power. That's a big

story. There are quite a number of examples like that around the world.

Some societies use the bullroarers to represent the voice of the deity. In one ritual, the boy is covered by the initiating man and then the bullroarers come. The man tells the boy that now the demon dragon, *Grandpa,* is coming to eat him. The kid thinks he's a goner for sure. That's the *Liebestod* idea that Wagner handles. You think you're dead and at that moment you've broken past it. All these initiation rites are based on the motif of death and resurrection. You think you're dead, really dead, and suddenly "bing," you've broken past it. You've got a new expanded life. What has died is the infantile ego.

You see, until a man is pretty well along, twelve to fourteen years of age, he is utterly dependent upon his parents and on his society. This causes a psychology of dependency to develop, a psychology of

submission, one of asking for approval but
expecting reproof. Then comes the problem of breaking out of that psychological
bondage into a self-responsible authority
with the courage to accept and express
your thoughts on your own life. This is
the problem of killing the infantile ego and
coming into the mature ego of authority.

Does this problem always present itself at pu-
berty or can it be delayed till much later in
life?

I always say that if you go through for your
Ph.D. you're in the dependency position
until you're thirty-five or forty and, in
fact, you may never get out of it. And, you
know, there is a very simple test! You can
judge by the number of footnotes a scholar
applies whether or not he's got his own
authority or is simply hoping that somebody will feel that he has the *right* authori-

ties. It's an important point, a sensitive point, in the academic world.

I remember one evening being impressed by the contrast of two interviews on the TV. In one, a professor was asked a question. He hemmed and hawed trying to get the answer out straight. And then a big league baseball player was asked a question. What authority he had! No hemming and hawing. He came straight out. He *knew*. He was an authority from the time he was playing ball on the sand lots. He asked no one's approval. That is the breakthrough to maturity, which is required to live the life of an adult.

What is the importance of the three goddesses, Circe, Calypso, and Nausicaa, in male initiations?

I came to the realization of the importance of these three goddesses in Joyce's *Ulysses*, in which Ulysses goes through the initiations of the goddesses. The Ulysses figure is Leopold Bloom. He goes through Dublin and encounters the nymphs Calypso and Circe—the poor mistress in the brothel is named Bella Cohen—and finally, the daughter. Mythologically, these are the roles that the female plays in the life of the adult male. And I think that in the lives of modern Western men these are the three main roles which females play for men after they have left the mother's house—not that men really get under the influence of these three. That's not it. Rather they have to accept the influence. I mean it doesn't do just to become involved in some simple seduction and then come out of it. You have to get the sense of what's happened. All these experiences are there for you to experience. If you don't really experience the sense of it, nothing's happening.

Now, the other initiation that is indicated in the *Odyssey* is the initiation of Odysseus's son Telemachus, who is in the mother's house. Daddy has been away for twenty years of wars and then lost at sea, and Athena, the goddess, comes and says to Telemachus, who is now twenty-two years old—he was two years old when Daddy left—"Leave your mother's house. Go find your father." Well, in myth this motif occurs, time and time again—"Who is my father? Go find your father." This means simply find your manhood. The young man has to break from the mother and find his action, his male action.

In rituals and in myths, most of the problems involved in finding male adulthood come about because the male has to intend to become an adult. It is different for the female. For the young woman, it happens to her. With her first menstruation she's a woman. Next thing she knows she's a mother. She doesn't have to work this thing out. It's working itself out on her and the problem of the woman is to realize who and what she has already become. The problem of the male, on the other hand, is to become what he can be. All the myths know this and all the myths build it up.

I remember reading what seemed to me a beautiful remark made by one of the men in the Mandan tribe, a tribe up in Minnesota. George Catlin, a young painter, went out from Harvard in 1832 and painted pictures of these Indians and the magnificence of their ritual and so forth. The young men who were hung up by spikes through their pectoral muscles and beaten said, "We have to learn to suffer in order to compensate for the suffering of our women." Life brings the suffering on the woman, and the man has to match it by imposing suffering on himself.

We're now hearing that in the jungle tribes of Brazil these initiations of breaking a man, smashing him, giving him pain, are called "the male menstruation." That is to say, something is now living through his life that's not simply his personal intention. This happens naturally with a woman. She lives a life of nature whether she wills or nils, and if she nils, then she doesn't have her life at all. But with the male, nature doesn't do this to him. Society does it, and life does it, and he's got to learn to live for something else besides his own little ego will. That's the sense of the mythic initiations.

I think that women are much more immediately the victims of the biology of the body than men. Women today have been sold a bill of goods by the male-oriented society which is stressing *achievement* rather than *being*. This can pull a woman off center in a very dangerous way, and then she recognizes it and goes into a tailspin.

How does she recognize it?

Well, I noticed this in my generation where women were beginning to go out of college into disciplined work in the arts. Now, this type of work takes everything you've got if you're going to be a major artist, and it is not a field in which women worked, in traditional societies. Work in this way requires a sacrifice of life. I think T. S. Eliot said that the career of a writer is a life crucifixion every day. I know that my own work of scholarship has been a disregarding of the claims of life and an insistence and dedication to the claims of my skill. Well, in those years when I was preparing myself, my sister and a number of other young women I knew were going strenuously into the arts, but then, as they approached thirty, a look came into their eyes and perhaps two out of three dropped it and made sudden bad marriages. They suddenly realized, "There's another claim on me." Men don't feel that way. Men don't get it that way.

There's a wonderful passage that Leo Frobenius has published of an argument that he recorded from the lips of an Abyssinian woman. She said, "I'll tell you why we don't listen to our husbands. What do men know? Whatever happens to them? When a woman has her first menstruation her total life is changed. When she has a child, she's split in half and, from that moment on, whether that child lives or dies, she's a mother. But what about men? From the time of their circumcision to their death nothing happens! That's why we don't listen to our husbands." And there's a big point there. You can see this distinction clearly in the puberty rituals in

traditional societies. The ritual for the girl
with her first menstruation was normally
just to sit in a hut and realize what was
happening to her, that she was now a vehicle of a transpersonal power. These things
were happening to her outside her own
personal wishes, and it was not up to her
to make decisions regarding them. So you
could say that life overtakes the women.
But the transpersonal power of nature
never overtakes a boy in the same way, so
in the traditional societies he had to be
broken into becoming a vehicle of something—not a vehicle of nature like the
girls, but a vehicle of the society. Typically,
mythologically, woman is the vehicle of
nature and man is the controller of society, but he has to control it in terms of
the social order and not his own personal
wishes. And when you think of what was
done to the young men! It's horrific the
way they were smashed up! They were not

the same thing they were before the initiation. They were totally transformed.

Would you give an example of the horrific ways the boys were "smashed up" in these rituals?

Well, in 1832 George Catlin went directly from Harvard to the upper Missouri River and with his paintbrush did a magnificent recording of the Indian tribes there, just about fifty years before they were knocked to pieces. He painted portraits of some of their great chiefs. Now, you've probably noticed that when you look at a straight-on portrait, the eyes seem to follow you. Well, when the Indians observed this in Catlin's portraits, they thought he was a magician, that he actually had done things that were alive in the eyes. They were so impressed that they gave him access to a number of inward rituals that no white man had ever seen. He witnessed them and painted many pictures. As well, he wrote letters in which he describes in detail the initiation rituals of those young men.

They were first taken into a great hut. Now, it's important to keep in mind that nobody had any choice about going through this ceremony. No one could say, "Hey, I'm not a warrior. I'm a peace man, you know." The boys were taken in and made to sit for something like five days without eating—if you've ever tasted, you know five days with no food does something to you. Then incisions were cut in their chests and wooden pegs about a foot long and two inches thick were pressed right through their pectoral muscles like skewers. Ropes were attached to the exposed ends of the pegs. More wooden skewers were then forced through their thigh and calf muscles, and heavy buffalo skulls were hung from these. Catlin says, and in his paintings he shows us, that when the pegs were being put through their muscles, these boys made a very special point of smiling and acting as though nothing were happening.

Then the boys, hanging by the ropes attached to the skewers through their pectoral muscles, were hoisted up to the roof of the hut. Each one held his medicine bag which was his special power resource. The men then beat them with long poles so that they spun around and around until finally they passed out. When all the boys were unconscious, they were dropped to the floor.

As soon as they began to recover, two strong men grabbed them, one on either side, and started running with them, first around the hut and then outside around the ceremonial field. They continued racing, hauling the boys between them, until the buffalo skulls eventually pulled out the

skewers from the boys' leg muscles. Then
the men dropped the boys. They were, of
course, utterly wiped out. The point of the
ritual was that the boys were to experience
death. That is to say, to experience a total
giving up, an experience of resting well in
God, of yielding themselves to the divine
power. Catlin tells of one boy who was
hauled around and around, but the buffalo
skull didn't pull the skewer out of his calf.
This youngster went running around outside the village until he finally hung himself by this skull from a tree that was hanging out over the Missouri River about one
hundred feet below. He thought his
weight would finally pull it out. Well, it
did, and he dropped into the river and
swam ashore. Those young men said to
Catlin at one time, "Women suffer. We
must suffer too." This is recognizing both
the continuity of the relationship of the
woman's experience, which overtakes her,

and the experience of the man in giving himself to the society.

Now, this is traditional stuff. But what's happening today is that women are not contemplating what's happened to them. Rather they are thinking, "Gee, I want to be a successful store manager or artist or professional." So they're sold the active role of the male instead of taking active delight in the *being* role of the female.

Circumcision is often a part of the puberty rituals. What is its symbolic significance?

The best interpretation I've read of circumcision has come from Africa. Circumcision is a ritual that belongs, I think—I'm not sure about this—to the tropics and also to desert people. In the Sudan there are a number of examples, not only of circumcision, but also of clitoridectomy, where there is an incision of the clitoris in the young woman. The idea is that they're born androgyne, male and female, and what the circumcision is meant to do, according to this interpretation, is to release the full manhood from occlusion in the mother womb. It's symbolically interpreted that way. Similarly, with the removal of the clitoris from the female organ, the male element is removed and the person is fully female. The ritual takes place at puberty.

Now, an interesting thing in the Jewish tradition, just like baptism in the Christian religion, is that it doesn't occur in puberty. It occurs in childhood. This means that society has taken you over and you're no longer the authority. The society is. In Judaism, circumcision has been given a very special interpretation as the sign of the covenant and this, of course, leaves the female out—I think Jewish females now, particularly in the women's movement, are beginning to feel this. But in the Sudanese rituals, and I think it's probably from Africa that the Jews got this, the ritual is that of coming to your full sexual maturity.

Where do we see initiation rites today?

Well, there are certain marginal tribes that still conduct these initiation rites. I believe some are still going on in Australia. I don't see much of it in any culture where the West has moved in in strength. I would think that in the Solomon Islands and in New Guinea these things would still be going on. I can't give up-to-date examples.

We have certain of these rites in our society. In Judaism the maturity ritual is the Bar Mitzvah of the boy. He's supposed to be a man from then on. Also marriage is an ordeal basically of losing yourself in a higher polarity, the androgyne relationship. I think one of the problems in marriage is that people don't realize what it is. They think it's a long love affair and it isn't. Marriage has nothing to do with being happy. It has to with being transformed, and when the transformation is realized it is a magnificent experience. But you have to submit. You have to yield. You have to give. You can't just dictate.

In Europe until the Second World War, military service was required of every young male for three years. That was the ritual. It wasn't intended as a rite, but that's the way it worked. In the Roman Catholic Church a confirmation is supposed to be that ritual. The Bishop, however, gives you a little swat instead of tearing you to pieces, so it doesn't work. Nothing happens. Also, if one goes into a convent, I mean seriously, one goes through a death and resurrection. Sometimes, there is an actual ritual enactment of a simulated death and you come up with another name. You are now Brother Felicitas instead of Mike Jones. The name is changed. The old characters are left behind and a new spiritual self is born. But, in general, our education has nothing to do with these rituals. Our education is mostly concerned with the communication of information and that's not enough. There's no real ordeal of transformation.

Does it matter that these puberty rites have been lost?

Sure! It matters very much that the puberty rites are lost, because without them men remain boys! In our society, instead of mature human beings, we have continuing adolescence — forty-year-old adolescents.

Where do you see that manifest in the men in our society?

It manifests itself in a good deal of "mother's-boyism" and in broken marriages. Also, I think homosexuality, in some forms, is a failure to come through to your manhood. Afraid to make the step. The female for the male represents life, and an infantile ego is afraid of this challenge. Think of Hamlet, for instance: "To be or not to be?" For goodness sakes, what a question! And what is his relationship with a woman? "Ophelia, get the hell out of here. Go drown yourself." Where you have the strong ascetic either in the way of a religious asceticism or of a homosexual asceticism—not responding to the polar game that's proposed—you have a failure to come through into life. And for the male, the female is life. She is the challenge of life.

5 · ANIMALS

ONE OF THE important principles in what might be called the pictorial vocabulary of mythology is the assignment of certain animals to certain roles. When the sun and moon have important symbolic powers, you find that certain animals do too. They are different in different places—in primitive America, Africa, and Europe. I'm going to talk about the Euro-Asian system where you have lions and bulls.

The moon dies and is resurrected. The moon sheds its shadow, as the serpent sheds its skin, to be born again. So it becomes associated with this problem of the principle of life involved in fields of time—death and rebirth. The sun, on the other hand, does not have a shadow within itself. It's always a crisis when the sun is eclipsed. Something has eclipsed it; the sun hasn't eclipsed itself. The sun is always radiant and so symbolizes the power of life in consciousness, disengaged from the vicissitudes of time. So we have these two ideas of eternity: the eternal principle involved in the field of time, which is associated with the moon, and eternity transcending and disengaged from the time principle, which is associated with the sun.

Obviously, the serpent shedding its skin and the moon shedding its shadow belong together. Now, they're associated with respect to the sun, which is represented by the eagle, the hawk, and the sunbird—the bird flies free from the bondage of earth and so represents this free flight. The serpent pounced on by the eagle is a motif you get in Mexico and in Greece. In Southeast Asia, the sunbird pounces on the serpent. It's a standard motif of the fire of the sun drying up the moisture in the world and killing it. The sun is a killer. It's the warrior—a solar figure. So this business of the relationship of the eternal to the temporal order is one that is symbolized in the polarity of these two principles—the sun both kills the moon and then becomes the mother out of whose womb the moon is born.

The animal associated with the sun in the Euro-Asian sphere is a lion with a solar face—many cats have been associated with this principle, but the lion is the great cat. Now, the animal on which the great cat preys is normally a grazing animal, an antelope or a bull in South Africa, and just as the lion pounces on the bull to kill it, so the sun pounces on the moon. So the horns of the bull and the horns of the crescent moon are associated. Now, the bull, in order to represent the moon, must die so that a young bull can take its place. And so, in cults where there are cattle, the bull becomes the primary sacrificial animal. Thus we have a solar/lunar, lion/bull, eagle/serpent polarity. This is the basic symbolism for this mystery of the relationship of the two eternities to each other — the bull representing eternity in the field of time.

Another animal that has this association in an earlier culture stratum is the boar, whose tusks are shaped like crescent moons. The black face of the boar lies between the dying moon and the resurrected moon just as three dark moonless nights separate the waxing and waning moon. In our calendar, Good Friday and Easter are associated with the moon. They are placed in relation to first full moon after the spring equinox, the solar/lunar coincidence. Also, Christ is three days in the tomb, as the moon is three days dark. Only then is the stone removed.

What has happened in all the dead and resurrected god mythologies is that the lunar symbolism has been taken over. In the Christian sacrifice, which goes back to the Semitic tradition, they did not have the bull but they had the sheep, the ram. So Jesus is the sacrificed lamb. In Egypt, the ram is the solar symbol. The creator is associated with the ram. All these associations are speaking the same old story of finding the eternal life in the temporal. That's the problem of our existence, you might say, to read through our temporal experience the eternal life that we are experiencing.

What's the symbolism of bullfighting?

Well, just look at a bullfight. The bullfighter is wearing a brilliant shining garment and represents the solar power, while the bull, of course, represents the moon power. In the bullfight, the point of danger, which leads to the coup de grâce, is the act of going in over the horns of the bull, which represent the crescent moon.

A similar ritual appears in relation to serpents. I once saw a marvelous film way back in the early forties or late thirties, which showed a Burmese priestess in northern Burma. She was a priestess of a serpent shrine in which the serpent was a king cobra. In order to bring rain, this woman had to enact the sacred marriage with this serpent by kissing it on the nose three times. It's very much like the bull-fighter going over the horns of the bull. You sacrifice the bull so that there should be a new period. The past must be killed so there can be a future. The movie is a fantastic thing to see. They used a tele-scopic camera, and you could follow the priestess going up the mountain to a cave. She makes a noise and out comes this cobra. You can see it. She fixes him, just as the bullfighter fixes the bull, then goes over and kisses the nose of this snake. You see the venom flying all over the place. She had to calm him down. She had to fix him three times. Then *snap,* and he goes back into his cave.

Another example of this same motif, the serpent and bull, occurs in marriage. Marriage is the killing of your separateness. You become one part of the larger unit. You're no longer the separate one. Also, we see the same motif in Egypt; after his death, Osiris begets his hero son Horus — when you have a begotten son, you become secondary. The son is primary, and you're there as a fostering presence. You are no longer number one. His birth is death to your primary existence. So these two things are linked up very strongly. Marriage and death, and birth and death ceremonies have a lot in common.

Are animal sacrifices still enacted today?

Well, the Spanish bull ceremony is one. And in Southeast Asia there are sacrificial bull ceremonies, real bull killings. And in India, think of the great ceremony of the goddess which occurs in September. It's fantastic! Not bulls, but hundreds of goats are sacrificed.

Is the symbol of sacrifice living in our culture?

The Roman Catholic Mass is supposed to be a literal reenactment of the Crucifixion, and the Crucifixion was the sacrifice to end all sacrifices. So I would say the sacrifice of the Mass can be understood as a continuation into the present of the mystery of the sacrifice. Now, this mystery is interpreted in various cultures from various points of view. Personally, I've always found it repulsive that animals had to be killed in order for a person to have a mystical experience. But it still goes on. I was once in India at the time of the temple sacrifice in Calcutta and I just couldn't stay to watch it, that's all. I don't want to see animals killed. I can tolerate it theoretically, but visually I don't want to see. And I don't want to see a bullfight. I've seen one and that's plenty for me. But some people seem to get some kind of spiritual thing out of it that I just don't understand myself.

Historically, when did humans become conscious that animal sacrifice was a projection?

The first important voice in our culture against sacrificing animals was that of Zar-

athustra, who saw this as an act of barba-
rism. In any real sense of the sacrifice, you
must sacrifice some aspect of yourself, and
if it becomes concretized in an animal,
then, instead of sacrificing your own animal nature, you sacrifice an animal.

Another view is that you're giving a
gift, a payment, so that the god will do
something for you. That's another reading.
This is one that Fraser brings out in *The
Golden Bough.* In northeastern Siberia the
only animals the people have are sled dogs.
I have a picture that I hope to use in my
next book of a whole field of sacrificed
dogs on spikes. These are the people's best
dogs. They don't sacrifice just their riffraff
dogs; they pick their best dogs and give
them as a sacrifice to a power, which then
will do something for them. This is a
purchase motif, the salesman/merchant's
theme. The mystical interpretation is the
sacrificing of something that you cherish

in order to release yourself from bondage to that cherishing position. And what you may cherish may be your animal nature or it may be just any good that you have. What's the sense of sacrificing one's oldest son or the youngest or second son? There was a lot of this that went on in many cultures. It's strange . . . strange. I think of it as a morbid development, which is a result of concretizing a mythological concept. You concretize certain aspects of your own nature in the external world, and then sacrifice them.

Now, where you have human sacrifices, very often that sacrifice is a giver of great power. For instance, when you sacrifice the animal, you absorb the power that has been given away. It's no longer out there, it's in you. One of the great areas for really wild sacrifice is in Melanesia, where the men in their secret societies raise pigs. They knock the upper canines out of their principal pig's jaw, so that the tusks can grow right around and come back through the jaw again. There are a couple of these skulls in the British Museum. With each important stage of development of that circling tusk, hundreds of pigs will be killed so that the big pig is absorbing the pig power, and the man who owns the pig changes his name. He's gained power through this sacrifice. It's a fantastic thing. When he gets to be a thirty-second degree mason, he can come into the meetings with his hands out as though he were fly-ing above time and space, and he'll have a name such as "he who walks above the sun" or something like that. He has gained the power along with the pig. Then when he dies, the pig becomes his sacrifice to the goddess who is on the road to the fire of eternal life, and instead of consuming the man, she consumes his pig. So the pig has become his savior. The pig is his savior and saves him for eternal life. This is the animal, you might say, as a signal in a spiritual disciplining and transformation of oneself. As one goes on, one learns more and more of the spiritual life through these sacrifices.

In this case the god, the personification of a transcendent power, is honored and brings about a positive transformation in human life. You spoke earlier about devils being a personification of energy which was not revered.

Right.

Can you tell us a myth or myths that reveal this personification of energy?

There is a figure in American Indian myths that represents this power of the dynamic of the total psyche to overthrow progress. This is the negative aspect and it's called a *trickster*. It's a very, very important figure in American Indian mythologies. In the forest lands of the Northeast and Southeast, the trickster is the great hare or rabbit. When you go west of the Mississippi in the plainsland, it is called *coyote.* You get up in the Northwest coast and it's *raven.* These are smart, clever birds and animals. Now, it's a great puzzler to well-trained Christians to come across the trickster hero because he's both a kind of devil and fool, but also a sacred creator of the world. And so he comes in as an upsetting factor. He breaks through. Sometimes he even breaks through the notion of what the deity ought to be, and this, I think, is about as good an example as you can find anywhere of the trickster hero. Now, that trickster trait turns up in deities like Yahweh. Yahweh's a trickster. He lets people build a building, and then because it gets to be three stories high and he's afraid it's going to wreck heaven, he comes down and floods the world. That's a trickster stunt. That's a ridiculous act. We think it quite normal for a deity, while if a human being behaved that way we'd send him to a lunatic asylum. The trickster represents the deity coming through as the destroyer, the disrupter of programs. Yahweh is full of this kind of thing.

Would you tell us a story about "coyote" or "raven"?

I suppose the most important myth associated with this trickster is that of the flood, the North American Indian flood. The story will start with all the animals on a raft with *old man,* who is a humanized aspect of *coyote.* After a certain time he sends a diving animal down, a muskrat, or a diving bird—a loon or something like that—to get a little piece of mud off the bottom and bring it up. The divers bring up the mud, and then the old man takes it and puts it on the water and makes some magic, and it gets bigger and bigger and bigger. Then he sends a fox or some other animal to run around the world to see if it's big enough, and on the third or fourth time, it is big enough and there we are— creation.

The theme of the old man on the raft is a little different among northern Siberians, the Finns and the Laps. Here, the diver is the shadow of god. In these stories the deity sends a diver down—it's known as the earth diver motif—and he comes up with a little bit of mud but he doesn't give it all to the deity. After the deity has put the mud down and made a perfectly orderly world, this other one spits out the rest of the mud and that makes mountains and difficulties. In later traditions where the cosmic order has been recognized—

the round of the stars—very often the planetary deities are regarded as tricksters because they introduce disorder. They move a different way and anything that is a disordering principle is associated with a trickster—the diabolical as opposed to the demonic.

Our interpretation of the word *demon* as meaning the demonic is a very interesting thing. The demonic comes from the Greek, and it refers to the dynamic of life—your demon is the dynamic of life. In our tradition we are so against the dynamic of life that we've turned it into a devil. *Demon* has negative meaning in our tradition. This is fantastic. Similarly, the serpent, which also represents the dynamic of life, has been turned into a negative principle in our tradition. The serpent can shed its skin to be born again, and so represents the power of life to throw off death and represents the bondage of life to time. It's the dynamic of life and consciousness in the field of temporal pairs of opposites, birth/death and all that, and life goes on through it. It's as though our tradition is against life. Even our deity himself is against life. We have a deity who talks about supernatural grace and virtue, but life itself is something to be despised instead of celebrated, and a body is something awful rather than awesome. It's a strange world.

Does the symbol of the winged fish unify these two aspects?

Well, there aren't many people in the world who know anything about winged fish. It can be seen in only certain parts of the ocean, so it's not a figure that appears very frequently in mythologies. Where it would appear, it would represent exactly the same thing as the feathered serpent.

That is to say, something that represents the abysmal, or the earthbound, or the waterbound that takes off and is in flight. So it combines the two principles of bondage to the earth and release from it. That's the important thing to realize in life. You don't have to be quit of your bondage in order to experience the release. The two go together.

How would that be experienced in an individual's life?

In an individual's life all this is really a great mystical experience. The individual no longer identifies himself with the history of his carnal body but with the consciousness that informs that body. When you are identified with the consciousness rather than with the vehicle, the bondage of the vehicle has nothing to do with the bondage of the consciousness. You are free in bondage. Mythologically, the shackles fall without ever leaving your wrists. This is the condition of what in Buddhist tradition is known as the *Bodhisattva,* the one whose being is illumination. He knows that in the world, in the field of bondage, the eternal power plays. And so you have this forming a joyful participation in the sorrows of the world.

You can't eliminate the sorrows of the world. Time involves sorrow, and if you're in the field of time, that is the experience of your carnal body. But that which is participating in this has another dimension, the eternal dimension, and it can joyfully affirm this. This is the way that St. Augustine reads the Crucifixion. Jesus came to the cross like a bridegroom to the bride. That's to say, you come voluntarily to eternity, participate voluntarily in the processes of time, which are of sorrow and death. And so he comes to the cross, which is the cross of life and time, voluntarily. When you get that affirmative aspect you've got a sense of Christianity that is heroic. The accent in our tradition, however, has been on Christ's suffering and our sins having poured their weight upon his shoulders, and this poor, poor man, how he suffered for you. That's not it! There's the other Crucifixion, of Christ triumphant, with his eyes open, voluntarily on the cross. That's where we all are, and when you can identify yourself with that myth, you're released. Do you see what I mean? This is the bird flight linked to the serpent bondage in one image.

When the ego is capable of that participation in the Crucifixion, then you are in the *imitatio Christi*. You really are in the imitation of Christ and you have achieved the goal, I would say, of the Christian message.

In psychological terms, you have spoken of the importance of developing an ego strong enough to sacrifice certain values and thereby transform itself. Would you comment on the ego's capacity for self-reflection and the role of mythology in this process?

Well, ego can't reflect upon itself unless it has a mirror against which to read itself, and that mirror would be the mythological schedule that lets it know where it is.

The myth is the reflection of . . .

No. The myth is the mirror from which the ego can see itself reflected. It's a mirror with a schedule on it, a patterned mirror, and the ego sees itself in that reflex and knows where it is on the scoreboard. Just as, for example, a person who, at the age of forty, is wondering whether he's going to be punished by mother hasn't moved on, and a person at the age of eighty who's wondering, "How's my golf score?" hasn't moved on either. I mean just in a raw, gross way, this is the problem.

How do the myths help with a solution?

The myth lets you know where you are. It knows what the patterns of life have been through centuries and what position you now are entering or holding.

So what should the forty-year-old and the eighty-year-old see?

The forty-year-old should see himself as an independent, self-responsible human being with free will. And he should have certain noble powers of the heart that have been called to his attention and to which he has been invited to give himself. That will enable him to act in terms of nobility, not in obedience, but out of himself. On the other hand, the older person must know, "I'm now not participating in the achievement of life. I have achieved it." Personally, in my own life I am now looking back, and I can tell you that there's a wonderful moment that comes when you realize, "I'm not striving for anything. What I'm doing now is not a means to achieving something later." Youth has always to think that way. Every decision young people make is a commitment to a life course, and, if they make a bad decision, by the time they get down the road they're far off course. But after a certain age, there's not a future, and suddenly the present becomes rich, it becomes that thing in itself which you are now experiencing.

How old are you now?

I'll be seventy-nine next month. I'm in that place where every experience is of value in and for itself without any reference to anything that might happen. I've mentioned this to older groups, and people have come up to me afterward and said they didn't realize this. It's very beautiful. I can think of a couple of Renaissance pictures of an old man and an old woman looking at a new-born child. These are the two eternities: the youth—the lovely young thing—and the old one who's not in history anymore. But in between there is history. We're participating in a historically conditioned culture, and part of the role of myth is to relate that historical conditioning to what the old man and the child represent across the ages of life.

Can life have meaning without myth?

It has the meaning even if you don't know
what it is.

What's the difference?

The myth helps you to know how to read
these things, that's all. The meaning is always there. Sometimes you can come to it
by yourself. Great poets come to it, so why
not you? Well, we're not all great poets.

6 · UNDERGROUND

M YTHS OF DESCENT into the underworld are of a descent into those
domains of your own psyche that you have
not been paying attention to. We live on
the surface of our own lives, and the mind
is aware of only certain interests and intentions, but the body has other potential-
ities, other interests, and so forth. Now,
when you shipwreck in the shallow waters
of your intellectual notion of what your
life's about, wherever you shipwreck is
where your depth is. Then you go down
into what old Frobenius used to call "the
night sea," down into your own abyss to
find there the forgotten, the omitted energy, which should have been informing

your life but which was being excluded by your conscious posture.

There are two ways of going into the underworld. One is by being swallowed, and the other is by killing the monster that guards the gate. In the former, being swallowed, the person is taken on the night sea journey unconsciously. The Jonah story, for instance, is a typical descent journey of this type. He is swallowed by a whale, which is the personification of the powers of the abyss. Now, the journey always includes going past a pair of opposites, the Symplegades—the rocks that clash together. They represent the pair of opposites of our way of thinking. There are certain moments in life when you can have insights that can go past the pair of opposites. It's as though you can see in that moment a deeper truth, as if the opposites open and you can see into the unknown. Well, the two jaws of the whale are exactly the pair of opposites. One goes through the jaws into the abyss. And you will notice, by the way, that Jonah came out of the whale an improved character.

There is also the dragon slaying motif, where the hero goes through the opposites by way of his own consciousness, instead of in the unconscious way of Jonah. Siegfried is an example of the dragon slayer. He must kill the dragon and taste the blood. The dragon is symbolic of one's own unconscious, and killing the dragon and tasting his blood means you've eaten and tasted the life energy, which is in your own unconscious and was formerly unknown to you. After Siegfried killed the dragon and tasted the blood, the world of nature spoke to him. He understood the language of the birds and the flowers. So you can go on an underground journey in two ways: one, like Jonah, where the unconscious seizes you and carries you down, the other, like Siegfried, by choosing to take an intentional voyage down.

The association of this dark sea voyage with the cycle of the year is a fundamental one, particularly in agricultural societies. You plant the seed and for a while it's in the underworld and then comes the fruit. If the seed doesn't die, then you don't have life. That is to say, it's not really the death of the seed, but rather the death of the form of the seed. The life that was informing it is suddenly rendered visible and effective and present.

Would you relate this to the myth of Hades and Persephone?

The story of Persephone is an enormously important work in the tradition of classical mystical thinking. First, it's associated with the agricultural world. According to the legend, Eleusis was the place in which agriculture originated. Well, that's the legend. It's not the actual historical fact. Eleusis, this wonderful shrine, was there for a couple of thousand years and then the Christians smashed it up—to go to Eleusis now and see what those Christians did is absolutely appalling!

Eleusis was the sanctuary where one meditated on the mystery of the death and resurrection associated with the cycle of the seed that is planted and comes to fruition in the life-sustaining wheat. Persephone and her mother, Demeter, are personifications of the energies of this continuing vitality. The daughter, Persephone, is lost, abducted by the lord of the abysmal waters. It seems like a meaningless ravishing but it has purpose. It's actually a ravishing for the generation of new life. It's a beautiful myth and is associated with an actual ritual where the individual Athenian who participated in the ceremony experienced the death and resurrection in himself. So, you see, these myths can be read either in terms of an agricultural context of the mystery of the planted seed and the new life, or in a psychological aspect, the mystery of the death of your present ego system and the coming through of a larger life in yourself.

This whole disappearance and reappearance of Persephone is the same elementary idea as we have in the death and resurrection of Jesus—dying to your mortality and being resurrected in your eternal character. Whether the personification is male or female is of secondary importance. The main thing is to understand what the spiritual message is. Whatever your horizon, whatever the walls of your city, they have to explode for a larger life to come in. I remember some French chef saying, "To make an omelette, you must crack the egg." And so it is if you want a larger form. You've got to break the smaller one without losing the energy.

This poses the problem of translating your own local inherited mythology, or religion, as we like to call it, into a cultural worldview, in order to see the essential meaning in the symbol—to see the earth from the moon, so to speak. In order to do that, the best way to learn is through comparative studies, to see how, for instance, the imagery of the Christ story and the imagery of the Buddha story are two local transformations of the same imagery.

This struck me in a very stunning way during the war with Japan. One of our New York newspapers published a picture of a photograph of one of the Japanese threshold guardians—those big military figures that stand threateningly with weapons. Underneath the picture it said, "The Japanese worship gods like this." Now, this is the kind of journalistic political thing that I think is worse than war itself because it's actually cutting yourself off from relationship to another culture. Well, they forgot to tell us something. They forgot to say that this guardian is one of two figures that guard a gate, and beyond the gate sits the Buddha saying, "Don't be afraid of those people. Come through to eternal life. I am seated under the tree of illumination and eternal life." Actually, in comparative viewing, those two guardian figures correspond precisely to the two cherubim that Yahweh put at the gates of paradise to keep you out. The tree of immortal life was in there. Man had eaten fruit from the forbidden tree and had thereby gained the knowledge of the duality of all things. So he was thrown out of the garden. And God said, "Now if man should eat the tree of immortal life, he would be as we are. Therefore, keep him out." And he placed the guardian figures, the two cherubim, at the gates to the garden. Now, the Buddha says, "Don't be afraid. Come on through. The tree's right here. Don't be afraid of those boys." Jesus went through and hangs on the tree of immortal life. Jesus and the Buddha are the same figure. The Buddha sits under that tree and says, "Don't be afraid." Christ hangs onto that tree and says, "Come, die as I've died to immortal life." It's wonderful the way these great images play across the ground.

It's interesting that in Japan when you look at these two guardians, one has his mouth open and the other has his mouth closed. They represent a pair of opposites—fear and desire. Your fear and your desire are keeping you out of the garden. Your fear of death and your desire for the goods of life are keeping you out of the realization of your immortality, which transcends all this. That's what the guardians symbolize. Now, in the biblical tradition the imagery of two cherubim doesn't tell you that the guardians represent aspects of your own psyche. It's as though the god just got angry and said, "Stay out of here."

I have a funny thought about the Jewish-Christian tradition. It all has to do with sin and atonement, with debt and payment. This is merchant stuff. When St. Paul preached to the Athenians, they laughed at him, but when he went to Corinth, which was a merchant community, he could establish a church—the Epistle to the Corinthians. Now, I see Judaism and Christianity as translations of the universal mythology into the vocabulary of merchants. It all has to do with sin and atonement, debt and payment; and the very word *redemption* has to do with redeeming pawn from a pawnbroker. St. Gregory brought this up. Satan got man in his keep by deceiving him in the Garden of Eden and God, to get man out of the devil's keep, offered his son as redemption. Now, this is good basic Christianity. That's one way of reading the Crucifixion. Why did Christ have to die on the cross? What's that got to do with anything? Well, one reading is that Christ is offered to the devil in redemption for the pawn that the devil had in his keep of man. The other is the atonement idea that God was so angry at this sin he could not be atoned. Man wasn't capable of atoning because man wasn't of a value comparable to that of the offense, and so God himself becomes man to rescue man. These two ideas, redemption and atonement, have to do with payment, and this is a merchant's reading of the great myths. Fantastic! All you have to do is read it back. This doesn't mean the merchant reading is wrong. It says simply that it's only one way of inflecting the myth, and if you're not thinking in those terms, then this doesn't mean very much to you.

This "underground" or "night sea" journey represents the way to break out of a limiting conscious posture into an expanded spiritual consciousness. Would you amplify that?

I think anyone who pays attention to his inner life knows when he is in harmony and when he's out of harmony with his center. If you're on the line, nothing can hurt you. I think it's Meister Eckhart who said "Love knows no pain." That is, "When you are living in a relationship to your love, nothing can damage that."

The Buddhists have a saying, "joyful participation in the sorrows of the world." Only then are you really in the field of life. Life isn't meant to be happy. That's not what it's all about. Ah, the damage that is caused by that attitude. All life is sorrowful. Sorrow is the essence of life. But can you handle it? Are you affirmative enough with your relationship to life to say "yea," no matter what? The extent of your power to say "yea" is the extent of your power to love, and when you begin to have hates, and when you begin to knock people down, and say, "No! No! This one, this Hitler, or Stalin, they're monsters!" then you have lost your bliss. They are manifestations of life too. Your limitation and understanding and experience is measured by the boundary of your love.

There's a saying in St. Paul, the Epistle to the Romans. When I read it I was preparing for a class on early Christianity, and I came across a line which seemed to me to cast the very essence of James Joyce's *Finnegans Wake,* which is a marvelously paradoxical thing. There's a number in *Finnegans Wake* that continually reoc-

curs — 11/32. It occurs as a date. It occurs
as a number of a patent. It also occurs as
an address, 32 West 11th Street. Now,
thirty-two is the number of falling bodies,
thirty-two feet per second, and eleven is
the renewal of the decade, so the Fall and
the Renewal motif are somehow there. In
any case, I read in Paul, "For God has con-
fined all men to disobedience that He may
show mercy to all." And I suddenly
thought, "By god, this is really the clue to
Finnegans Wake." It's God's will that you
should disobey, so that the other principle
of mercy should come in. I wrote down
the line from Paul and the reference. It
was Romans 11:32.

Do you get the ambiguity of this thing?
Bliss is the ability to absorb the horror of
that message, of that truth. The sort of
thing that is going on in Israel now has to
do with the affirmation of life. Life's that
way. Life's a killer. The question is, "Does

your love absorb it?" It's a terrible message and yet it's the bliss message. Bliss absorbs pain. But it's certainly not happiness.

That is obviously not the usual meaning of the word bliss.

This whole idea of *bliss* that I've been talking about is not an easy one to explain. If one associates it with happiness as opposed to unhappiness, one gets on the wrong track, because it includes the unhappiness system.

Let me give you an example of what I mean. I have a friend who is constitutionally in great pain. She has a bone disease that has involved an experience of great pain throughout her life. I remember talking to her one time about these things and remembering Nietzsche's phrase *amor fati*—loving your fate. Nietzsche says that if you say "no" to a single important factor in your life, then you've unraveled your entire life, because life is a context of formally integrated and related contexts. On the basis of this phrase, I said to this woman, "You've got to say 'yes' to this. This terrible pain that's with you all the time is your guru, your teacher. This is what has honed you into the beautiful person you are, and your pain and suffering is what builds your life and your character, and somehow or other you have affirmed this from the very beginning. You act and live as though you have said 'yes' to this from the start."

I know others who have had really serious sorrows come into their lives. If they can take this positive attitude and absorb it, the bliss experience comes out, and they then realize that what they're affirming is the whole structure of their life. It's an opportunity. It's the incarnation that they've taken to experience—the miracle

of this consciousness and the world that
they're in. It's very different from saying,
"Ow! This hurts. I'm going over there."
Very, very different. It's the joyous affirmation of the sorrows of the world. First,
you must experience those sorrows as
your own sorrows, and then, when you
have affirmed those sorrows, you come
into bliss. Anyone can try it. It's to find
where your pain is and by saying "yes" to
it, the whole new consciousness will suddenly be experienced. You'll be "saved," as
they say.

I have a little formula I give to my
friends who are asking me the way to live,
so that you're never against the wrong
wall. I say to follow your bliss, wherever
your true inner bliss is, wherever you feel
in harmony. And if you get off—as you
surely will—and you know you're on the
wrong road, hunt back, find your track,
find your bliss. And, you know, even with

people in middle life who have got to the top of the ladder and found themselves against the wrong wall, let them think where their bliss is. Is it fishing? Okay, then buy a fishing line. Wherever it is, follow it! And that starts it going.

Carl Jung had this interesting experience back in 1909 or '10. This is where he really got his message. He was writing a book based on the dreams and hallucinations of a woman who was in a complete schizoid crackup. She was not one of his patients. And he recognized that these dreams and hallucinations were precise counterparts to certain myths. So he wrote an exciting book—it was the book that told me all about it—in which he shows the comparison between the mythological and the personal image systems. The name of the book is *Symbols of Transformation*. When he finished that, he thought, "Now I know the difference between a life that is moved by a myth and a life that is not." And he said, "I asked myself by what myth I was living and I found I didn't know. So I proposed to myself that the goal of goals of my life would be to find by what myth I was living." And, of course, he wondered how he could go about this. Then he asked himself, "What was I absorbed by as a little boy, so absorbed that I didn't know the time was passing?" Well, he remembered how he played with stones, making little cities out of stone. So what did he do? He bought himself a piece of property and began moving stones around, building himself a little castle to activate his imagination, and he wrote down the images that came to him. He painted them and while illustrating these things he found what his myth was. He found his myth and it gave a joy and dynamic to his life right to the very end. He could suffer without real frustration all the abuse that he got when Freud turned the guns of character assassination against him after their separation— accusations of insanity and all this kind of thing. Jung took it, for he knew where his dynamic was.

You mentioned the "merchant" inflection of Christian mythology—debt/repayment, sin/ atonement. What are some other inflections?

Well, there's an aspect to mythology that is important to realize. The people of a culture get their messages from their priests and visionaries, and the priests and the visionaries may manipulate the myths to their own political advantage. In India, for example, the manipulation gave all the advantage and spiritual power to one caste, the Brahmans, and the idea of the spiritual life can be translated into, "That's the life, and we live it, and others don't have it."

Now, in the biblical tradition, you have a political manipulation that way also. After the Flood the first thing Noah did was to plant a vine. Then he got drunk, and as he lay drunk with his sex exposed, his son Ham sees him and says to his brothers, "Look at papa!" Then, Japheth and Shem, Noah's other two sons, bring a blanket and cover their father's nakedness—You know, there's something funny about people who live in deserts. They're ashamed of their bodies. I mean why should it matter that Daddy was exposed?—Anyway, when Noah realized what had happened, he decrees that Ham, who saw his father's nakedness, will be the slave of his brothers. Shem, who was the one who had the idea of covering the father's nakedness, will be the teacher. And Japheth, the goyim—who is all the rest of us in the world—will live in the tents of Shem. That is to say, Shem, the Semites, will be the instructor of our spirit, and Ham, the poor African, will be the servant of Shem and Japheth. This myth was a justification for black slavery. For many, many, many generations, this myth was used as a racial political distortion, you might say.

Another way of distorting a myth is to translate it into magic. Now I don't know what to say about magic because I've had enough experiences here and there to know that what we call magic sometimes works. The mystery spoken about in myths refers to the spirit, but since the spirit is a personification and a mode of experiencing the dynamics of life, perhaps there is one kind of echo which influences outer nature. It may be. It just may be. However, that can be over-emphasized and then you have again the pathology of myths. There are two pathologies. One is interpreting myth as a pseudo-science, as though it had to do with directing nature instead of putting you in accord with nature, and the other is the political interpretation of myths to the advantage of one group within a society, or one society within a group of nations.

Historically, many cultures believed that the unconscious energies of the body were revealed in dreams, and that dreams could be used for healing the body.

Yes, dreams reveal the energies of one's own body and show clearly when and how the energies get out of harmony. At these times, of course, one can become sick. This is the psychosomatic base for disease, and with certain diseases, if one can put oneself back in spiritual harmony again, the disease disappears. I know people who have had this happen even with cancer—a spontaneous remission from cancer as a result of certain kinds of meditation and thinking. Past traditions knew that when you're full of anxieties, something's gone wrong in your inward life. Then find out who the god is that you're not giving messages and sacrifices to, and you'll straighten yourself out.

There were wonderful sanctuaries in Greece, like Epidaurus, where people used to go for cures. The deity was Asclepius, who is the Lord of Medicine to this day—and, by the way, his principal animal symbol is the serpent, which represents the dynamic of life in the world, sheds its skin to be born again, and also represents the character of life. Life lives on life. You must realize you wouldn't be alive if you weren't killing, or somebody weren't doing the killing for you at every meal you eat. This is an important fact about the psychological relationship to the inevitable in life. Anyway, at Epidaurus, people's principal concern was first to eat a wholesome diet, have massages to put them in touch with their body again, and then sleep in the presence of the deity. Their dream would then tell them what was wrong.

I've seen—and I can't tell you what the reference might be—a beautiful votive panel thanking the deity for a cure. One picture shows a couch with a young man on it, and out of his own body comes a serpent that is licking or biting his shoulder. Then beside this picture another shows the young man asleep, dreaming. He has the dream of the serpent. The third picture shows him visiting the god, and the god is touching his shoulder in exactly the same place that the serpent did. The symbolization takes the form of an outer presence. But what is being symbolized is an energy from within yourself, which again can be symbolizing the form of the serpent power, the energy that transforms the life. Remember, the staff of the medical profession is of the two serpents coming and doing the job in two aspects. It's a symbol—the personification of the energy. The fact is you've cured yourself.

When you read a myth, it carries you forward and takes you into what I would call the spiritual life. You won't end up against the wrong wall if you follow your dreams as the signs of where your bliss is properly located.

7 · CONFLICT

I T'S HARD FOR US today to realize the
perilous situation of the early people in
the cultures of the Near East. For the
Western world, the beginnings of both
agriculture and the domestication of animals begins there. The first signs occur
somewhere around 10,000 BC. We begin
to see the domestication of some of the
animals of the neighborhood, principally
sheep and goats to begin with, and then
the pig comes in. Now, there may have
been an earlier beginning in Southeast
Asia. The finds that are taking place now
in upper northern Thailand are really
spectacular in transforming our picture
of the origins of agriculture. But, for the history of civilization in the Western world,

this area of the Near East is crucial—decisive.

Up to, let's say, 10,000 BC, all people were foraging nomads, hunters, and root and vegetable gatherers. Around that time the idea of cultivating their own food began to take place. As a result of this, increasingly large communities began to build up, and with the more substantial and dependable economic base came a whole new problem of cultural organization. People began to specialize, specialization in tilling the soil, in trading for goods with other centers, and specialization in governing these enlarged communities— the problems of organizing the community.

Now, the organized community, the viable unit, consisted principally of four castes: the governing, the priestly, the trading and merchant peoples, and the toiling peasants. These were coordinated around a spiritual center that represented the point that they were all serving—although they were differently trained, they all served the same center. And the city itself became what we're calling today a mandala, a sacred circle with a center to which everyone was related.

Now, there were two different developments, which came from early agriculture and the domestication of the animals. In the river landscape, in the high mountain valleys where it was possible to raise crops, the accent was on agriculture; in the broad grazing lands, the accent was on animal domestication. And so you have herding people—and there is a distinct separation, as early as the eighth and seventh millenniums, between the simple agriculturalist and the nomadic herding people. Where you have herders, the male is the important person. He's the one that is rounding up the animals, that is killing the animals, and protecting his herd from predators. There you have a warrior accent. But when the toiling is agricultural, the relationship is to the earth, which is the mother. She brings forth life and she nourishes life, and so the female principle is the dominant one there.

In this Near East zone, there were several main groups of people in these divisions. One was the people in the riverlands and the high valleys, agriculturalists, whose principal deity was the goddess, the world mother. The others were the two great herding communities. One was in the north, in southern Europe — the Indo-Europeans. They were herders of cattle and the domesticators of the horse. They invented the war chariot and became people of tremendous military power. The other community was the people of the Serbo-Arabian desert, the Semites. These were herders of sheep and goats, and later, the domesticators of the camel, which became the war camel—I think the earliest representation of the camel that we have in literature is in the Old Testament, where Rachel comes to Abraham on a camel. So we have these two warrior peoples fighting on relatively peaceful settled areas, and we find around the sixth millennium BC that the little settled communities begin to have walls and protection against these warrior people who were tough fighting, ruthless people, whether Indo-European or Semites. Read about Jacob and his tribe of twelve boys and one daughter and the city of Shepton. It was wiped out. Read the book of Judges. It's perfect for the period. This would be around the second millennium BC, the early or middle times of the second millennium BC. Yahweh tells them to go in and let nothing be left alive when you're through with it.

Then the Assyrians got the idea that when you wipe everybody out, you don't have anybody left to work for you. So, instead of wiping the people out, they transferred them to another place and brought people from that place into this place. This caused an enormous shuffling of people in the Near East so that all roots were broken. And, if this system had not been in effect when Jerusalem fell in the sixth century BC, the Jews would have been wiped out. Instead they were moved to Babylon. That was the principle that was used there. You'd save the people and enslave them.

Well, if the domestication of animals was the first really formidable and basic transformation, the second was the founding of cities and the invention of writing. As far as we know, the earliest cities in the world were those of early Mesopotamia, coming around the fourth millennium BC,

say about 3200 BC, something like that—
the cities of ancient Sumer. There you
have a professional priest caste. They invented writing. They used it first for simply recording gifts to the temple and so
forth, but then also for recording their ob-
servations of the heavens. Observing the
heavens was very important because that
was how you determined planting time.
You reap when crops are ripe, but in order
to plant one must know the heavens perfectly. As a result of recording observa-
tions of the heavens, it was presently realized that the planets, which formerly had
been thought of as a disturbing influence,
moved at a mathematically determina-
ble rate through the fixed constellations.
And here we begin to get mathematical
mythologies where certain numbers,
enormous numbers, begin to become very
important. Numbers like the number

432,000, which occurs in all kinds of relationships.

And then a total transformation of mythology takes place among "primitive" people. I use the word respectfully. I mean those who were there before writing came in and before this whole city development. They were close to the ground and close to nature, and special attention usually was given to exceptional objects: this exceptional animal, this exceptional tree, this particular place. These would become objects of worship. But when you begin to get the notion of a cosmic order, it's a totally new idea. Let's say the inevitable order takes over—and that there is an inevitable order is the basic mythology of all high cultures: the round of the sun in the cycle of the day and the year, the round of the moon in its cycles, the rounds of the planet Jupiter and the speed of its passage. At this time, the star Venus becomes very important for the Mayan and Aztec people. The realization that the evening star and the morning star were the same star was such a tremendous realization that they associated the god with that fact. So you see, when writing is introduced to a culture, the mathematical observation of the order of the heavens, all the powers of the order of the cosmos, become tremendously important.

It's at this time that we begin to have scriptures, which were rendered in terms of the needs and cosmology of that people, the notion of and order of the cosmos connected to a particular time and place. These scriptures were then handed to people who moved to a different location and lived in a different time. As a result, the scriptures were no longer relevant to the needs and cosmology of that people. This is how the scriptures have been passed down to us and why they throw us out of

touch with our own life. It's one of the
great misfortunes of the scriptural tradition. They petrify, crystallize, a myth in
terms of that particular culture at that
particular time.

This is true in our tradition where these
scriptures are carried from the Near East
of, let's say, 500 BC into our world today,
and explains why we have the notion of a
conflict between science and religion.
There's no conflict between science and
religion. There's a conflict between science
of the twentieth century and that of the
first millennium BC, which consisted of the
three-level universe in this tiny little world
and no notion at all of peoples elsewhere.
For instance, the Polynesians or the Chinese or the Hindus: there is no notion of
these at all in the scriptures — just Shem,
Japheth, and Ham. And what about the
Holy Land? That the Holy Land should be
somewhere else? That's ridiculous. The

Holy Land is here. As Black Elk said, "The central mountain of the world is everywhere." This is it! This is the Holy Land and you feel it is but no one tells you the gods are here. But they are. They're the personification of the energies of this place and if you know that, then you can put yourself in harmony with your own land.

One of the lovely mythologies to give us the sense of the importance of the land is that of the Navaho Indians in the deserts of New Mexico and Arizona. A totally different landscape and every element of that landscape, the red ant, the fly, the sunbeam, the rainbows, have all become personified. The people are realizing the spiritual presence everywhere. That's very different than the rest of us. We have to go to Israel for our Holy Land. People go on expeditions. Ridiculous!

The other day I was reading a hymn to the Indian god Shiva. It was a hymn of a person who had gone on pilgrimage to Benares, Shiva's city, and it read, "O Lord, I am guilty of two sins. One, I have made a pilgrimage to your city forgetting that you are everywhere; two, I am praying to you with words forgetting that you are beyond the reach of words." We've lost that! The words are in our scriptural texts and the Holy City is not everywhere. It is somewhere else, and it certainly isn't here.

This business of mythologizing your land, mythologizing the details of your life, they're totally different details from those of the first millennium BC in the Near East. The only people who can do it for us are poets and artists. The scriptures themselves come from the visions and realizations of poets and artists, but all the poets and artists that I know (and I know a lot of them—I've been living with them now for god knows how long), are at sea. They're at sea because the traditions don't tell them that their inspirations come from a divine transcendent source. Very few of them know how to break through, very few. They think studio problems are what it's all about, organizing the canvas, or writing a poem with certain use of words, in certain ways, in certain lines, and all that kind of thing. But that's not the problem at all. And it's a pity that our visionaries have been deprived of the realization of how important they are and what it is they're talking about—that poetry comes from a transcendent source. My God, the poet who realized this was Yeats, which probably makes him the greatest poet of the first half of the century. And James Joyce knew all about it. This is the hundredth anniversary of Joyce's birth, so I've gone back to reread him with what I have learned since I first read and wrote about his work. God, what he knew! And what he put into those books!

What was life like in the walled city?

The life in the walled city came right up through the fourteenth century in Europe, little cities like Rotenberg. In those days, the city was your life. It was your defender. You were born into it. It nourished you. It held you together and the people in that city constituted a dynamic living unit. It was very different from a metropolis of today, where you have people of totally different origins who come in to exploit the metropolis, and if they don't get what they want, then they get nasty and become vandals. They are dangerous in the city. You didn't get that in the old walled city. In a walled city everybody realized that the city was their life, and they were defending themselves and their life against enemy influences from without.

People are worried about atom bombs now! All the bomb can do is kill you and all your friends and everything associated with your life. Well, that was happening every weekend in those days. Cities were wiped out totally by invading people. People were living right on the edge of death all the time and this was true even in the Middle Ages. You had the Vikings coming down from the north; the Muslims coming up from the south; you had Indonesians fighting between this and that overlord. People's lives were right on the edge all the time. We've lost that. We no longer realize that life depends upon defense as well as on love. We've forgotten what our teeth are for. Not just to smile. They are there to kill! And this is a basic ingredient in life and an ability of life too. You have to be in form. Spengler's definition of a nation is "a folk informed for war." In that sense Israel is a nation and we are not.

Now, with respect to moving from one place to another and resanctifying the land, one of the most interesting examples of this problem and process occurred when the Norwegians went to Iceland. They brought their own mythology with them. It's the same thing with the Navaho. The Navaho are Athabaskan people. They came down into that area around the eleventh or twelfth century AD from northwest Canada, and they adapted themselves to the land. But they also adapted the land to themselves by bringing their myths with them.

There's a term in Icelandic, *landnom* — the *nom* is related to the German word, which means taking or claiming the land. You do this by mythologizing it, by recognizing, "We have brought our myths with us. We have the center, the center of the mountain of the world, the northern mountain, the eastern, the southern, the western. This will be the center. This will be the northern mountain. This will be the southern mountain." You name the land realizing that this is metaphorical. "The deities associated with the east—the rise of the new sun and the new day—we shall think of them when we look at the eastern mountain. Those of the gold and blue noon, the full blossom of the day, are to the south. The sunset, the mysteries of death are to the west. And that dangerous area when the sun is going back, the land of demons, to the north." Humans mythologize the whole landscape that way. That's what the Navaho did. That's what the Icelanders did. But we haven't done that here. People try to do it by naming cities after cities in the Old Testament, Canaan and all that sort of thing. But that doesn't work. That refers us only back to the Old Testament, not transcendence. So there's one of the problems about moving from one place to another.

Now, the next thing is that every living

mythology has grown up within a
bounded horizon at a certain time, in a
certain place, for certain people. Even
what we think of as world mythology.
These are not really world mythologies or
religions anymore. Christianity isn't a
world religion. It's only a religion of one
crowd against another crowd. And Judaism, of course, is a tribal religion still. You
can have intellectual walls as well as physical walls, and when you wall in your group
against another group you've walled yourself into a safe spot. But maybe it isn't so
safe. What's happened in the present
world is that there are no bounding horizons anymore. They've all been smashed.

My God, you can go from San Francisco
to Japan—which used to be a far, far dis-
tant, alien, unknown world—you can go
there in a day on an airplane. These
boundaries are gone. Yet we're still hanging on to the damn things! You know, the

way to get up against the wrong wall is to get up against the wall that isn't there anymore. You thought it was protective, but all it is is confining. This is happening all over the place. Now, you can't blame anybody. These transformations have happened within the last hundred years, just a little longer than my lifetime. I've seen it. When I was a kid, we never saw Chinese people who weren't laundrymen with pigtails down their backs. I never saw a Hindu until 1933 on a boat going to Europe. Now, however, these people are your classmates or members of your faculty on every campus. The old horizons have broken down, and if there is to be a world mythology, it's got to be of no particular time and place, of no selected people. Look what's happening! Look at the challenge that the planet is giving us now that the human community is the whole planet—including even our enemy the Soviet Union.

The world is one world, but everybody's pulling back into his own little group: black power, chosen people, the workers, capitalists, everyone fighting for his own small walled city. Well, the walls are down. There is no problem knowing what the themes of myths are. They've been the same everywhere. They are a constant system of returning archetypes that appear in all the mythologies, and we know what they are. The problem is the application of them.

One of the functions of mythology is supporting and validating the moral order of a certain given society. Well, what's your group? What's the society with which you associate? Is it this little in-group? Is it that little in-group? Are you hanging onto something from the third millennium BC or can you accept this challenge of the present moment? Open up and don't be afraid to let down the walls and let your neighbor in, so that you aren't defending yourself and your crowd against another system.

The key is the individual, not the social group anymore. All social groups are bounding groups now, and all social movements are in-group movements, walled-city movements. It's only the individual who can move from one group to another, and find the human spirit within himself, for whom we have any hope. I see nothing coming out of any of the social movements except in-group stuff—economics and politics. They talk about love but they don't mean it. An interesting example, of course, was the early pilgrims coming over to America. Freedom of religion was their main point. But what did they do? They immediately suppressed the Indian religions. The Indians were not allowed to practice their religions until only a couple of decades ago.

I remember when the meditation thing started, I was living in New York. The U.N. is there. Well, there were a lot of pious little people who were going to have a meditation room at the U.N. They said, "We'll have a meditation room which won't reflect any religious commitment — just a plain cross."

The walls are down, my friend, and it doesn't do to put a lot of these things around — crosses, and stars of David, and crescents, and all that kind of stuff. We don't have a symbol. As soon as you put up a symbol, you've got a commitment to something that's no longer functioning. The only possibility is to have a circle with all of the elements oriented to a void. You see, the center's everywhere.

There's a saying from a thirteenth-century book called *The Book of the Twenty-*

four Philosophers. It's a translation into Latin from an early Greek hermetic text and it says exactly what Black Elk says when he said, "The central city, the central mountain, is Harney Peak in South Dakota, but the central mountain is everywhere." This text says God is an intelligible sphere—intelligible means known to the mind—whose center is everywhere and circumference nowhere. So when you put a center and a circumference, that is a metaphor. It's not to be concretized. Your loyalty to your people is your loyalty to humanity through your loyalty to your people. That's the only way to get past this thing.

8 · FREEDOM

I THINK SHAKESPEARE said, "Life is a dream." But there's a beautiful paper by Schopenhauer called *On an Apparent Intention in the Fate of the Individual.* It's a lovely paper. He says that at a certain stage of life, when you're well along, you look back and it seems as though your life has been composed by a novelist. It has an order. It has a continuity. You suddenly realize that events which at the time seemed to have been just chance meetings actually played an important part in the structuring of this plot. And just as other people played these roles in your life, so you must have played equivalent roles in their lives, like a symphony of interlocking lives, or a Dickens novel—the characters cross and disappear, then, four hundred pages later, you suddenly realize the importance of that chance meeting.

But who is the author of our lives? Who is the builder of this interlocking dream? When Schopenhauer comes to this image he says, "It is *as if.*" He doesn't say, "It is." And that's very important! The great mythological point of view is, "It is *as if.*" He says, "It is as if the world were a dream of a single dreamer in which all the dream characters dream too, as if everything interlocks with everything else like the instruments in a symphony."

We have the same insight also from the Orient. Chuang-tzu's wonderful saying that's frequently referred to, "I dreamed I was a butterfly dreaming I was a man." We are all manifestations of an energy that we don't control and our life is, as it were, a dream.

Now, in the basic Indian Upanishad

thinking, there are four different levels of
consciousness. First, there is the level of
waking consciousness, where you and I are
solid bodies separate from each other. We
change form infrequently and we need illumination to be visible. But when we go
to sleep, we enter another world of consciousness, another world of relationship—the images of our dreams. This
world has a totally different logic, a non-
Aristotelian logic. In dreams, I am the subject looking at an object, but I am also the
object. The subject and object, which seem
to be two in waking consciousness, are
really one in dream consciousness. Here
we need no illumination. These bodies are
luminous, self-luminous. They shine. This
is the realm of deities and gods and myths,
the realm of the radiant body, the bliss
body.

Then beyond that level of consciousness, there is deep, dreamless sleep where

your consciousness is not aware of the consciousness that's moving your body. You're still a conscious body. Your heart's beating, and if it gets chilly you pull the blankets up over yourself, but you're not aware.

And then there is what's known as the fourth, when you go into that room of deep dreamless sleep, awake, and come into the experience of absolute consciousness. Not consciousness of any thing, but the consciousness of which all consciousness is a manifestation or modification. That is the mystery of the big total dreamer.

Now, we look as though we're separate from each other but we're not. We're two manifestations of the same life, and when life meets itself in contention or in erotic relationship, it's the one life in two persons. This is the dream realization—the mythological images like the Janus figure

of two faces or the androgyne of two sexes
and all they represent. The serpent biting
its tail. Life consuming itself. That is
what's going on all the time. It's the same
life in two aspects, eating itself, and to experience life that way is to move one stage
deeper into the mystery than the way we
usually experience life, as separate, economic man in relation to each other, getting benefits and losing benefits.

*How do you distinguish between the night
dream and the daydream?*

The daydream comes from a rationally con-
ceived intention of some kind. It's dealing
with something that the intellect, the rational mind, has proposed to the fantasies. It's a
free fantasy. Whereas the deep dream comes
right out of what I call the wisdom body
itself, the organs and energies that inform
our lives. And the intellect can't interpret it.

You have to have a psychiatrist, or someone who knows something about dreams, to come and tell you what it is that you've been trying to say to yourself. These deeply founded and grounded and energized dreams come from the same place that myths come from. This is the vocabulary of the living wisdom body. I have a little formula I use in my own thinking. Myth is the social dream and dream is the individual myth. By following your dreams you can discover the realm dynamics of your life course, your life intention, and your life impulse. Your mind can then furnish the implementation to achieve these aims and ends. Otherwise, one's living from the head.

This society tends to ignore dreams. Has this been true of other societies?

Well, all the traditions that I know about, except ours, respect the dream as information, which comes from that transcendent zone from which our very life has come. It's a message to us from that source. They also realize that that is also the source from which the myths come for the multitude.

Now, myths don't just come pouring out. The old romantic nineteenth-century philosophers and scholars in Germany had the idea that the people produce the myths. Well, they don't! Myths come out of an elite mind like Black Elk's, whose dream then becomes a source of rituals. Myth has always come from visionaries, and all the traditions tell us this. For instance, the whole mythos of the Biblical tradition was supposed to have come from Moses, not from the Jewish people. It was he who brought it down from the mountaintop. In the Old Testament, every time the people got into trouble, Moses went into himself, had a conversation with God, and then returned with more information. The leader is the spiritually motivated person, and insofar as a person's or a visionary's dreams correspond to the dynamic of his people, that's to say insofar as he is part and parcel of that life, his dreams will inform the life of the people. But you see, what's happened in our world since the nineteenth century is that the tradition itself is no longer spiritually motivated. Today, it is economics and politics, and the visionary is in another territory, and his visions come as strange to the people. This is the separation of the visionaries from the people, and the separation of the individual from the folk destiny, and that's what happens in a late culture when the accent has become economic and political.

You can see this by just viewing cities and towns. Look at a medieval city. The highest building was always the cathedral. Go down to the old towns in Guatemala and you will see that the highest buildings were the temples. But when you come to seventeenth-century Europe, the principal building is the palace. The culture has moved to a political center. Approach any one of our cities, San Francisco for instance, and what do you see? What are the highest buildings? They are economic buildings, either high apartment houses or office buildings. And that tells you what's running the culture. This shift of accent is what's known as the end of the culture. Spengler in *The Decline of the West* saw this, that our culture is in the stage of early Rome. The beginning of the end is the utilitarian, politically organized state. Now, Augustus Caesar had the wit to transform the old agrarian myths into Roman myths, which celebrated the Roman state. But we haven't had anybody who's done that for our material yet, and so we don't have any spiritual links to what we're doing.

We have great freedom and that's a blessing. What must happen is that some mythological instruction should be added to our freedom, so that the individual can find his own myth, his individual meaning in that freedom. It would be a shame to go back to the Middle Ages where everybody had to believe in the same myths. This is what Russia has done. I don't know why they call this progressive. It is regressive. Each individual must have the same faith, otherwise he can't live in the culture. The great thing about an open society is that it realizes that part of the culture is economic/political but, at the same time, it allows the individual to find his own spiritual dynamic in his own way within that culture field. Society doesn't work against him. But, according to what one sees coming, this is a moment that's not going to last very long. This is our great moment.

Do you mean that on a world basis, the god who is not revered will blow this culture to pieces?

Sure! I mean these are the dynamics of the spirit and the spirit is what runs civilizations. It's the human life. It's the energy of life and when only a certain system of energy is given validity and is listened to, the rest is there to explode it. Now, there was something wrong in Europe back there in the beginning of this century. I mean a little assassination at Sarajevo and Europe explodes into war. What's the matter? Europe has knocked itself out in two wars of insanity. The Greeks did the same thing—the Peloponnesian War, Sparta against Athens. They knocked themselves out, and then came Alexander the Great.

And you see North America doing this too?

There's no doubt about it. Nobody knows what to say because nobody knows how to read a symbol.

Why has our culture gone this way?

Well, as a culture gets to be more and more complicated, the simple mechanics of life become more and more complicated, and finally they absorb all the attention of the people. I am not in a position to say *why* this happens but *that* it happens is evident in front of our eyes.

At the end of the last century and the first of this, there lived a very great German anthropologist named Adolf Bastian. He was a wide traveler as well as an an-

thropologist and medical man, and he recognized that throughout the world the
same mythological symbols occur: death
and resurrection, virgin births, promised
lands, and all this kind of thing. He called
these "elementary ideas." Carl Jung, the
Swiss psychiatrist, came in on this discov-
ery by asking the important psychological
question, "What is it in the human psyche
that supports and makes for all these symbols and motifs being found everywhere
throughout the world?" It was Jung who
called them archetypal images, *arche* being
an all-enclosing type—a type that is
found everywhere.

And Bastian had another observation.
These elementary ideas appear in different
forms and with different interpretations in
different parts of the world at different
times, and he called these "folk ideas"—
the folk idea being a folk inflection of the
elementary idea. In our world today, all of

us are stuck to our folk inflection of the elementary idea, but all we have to do to have a world culture is to turn our *folk* into a metaphor for the *elementary,* to realize the universal humanity in your folk tradition, which isn't peculiar just to you.

A typical example of the archetype in mythology is the elementary idea, which appears in different folk forms and the different traditions, in the Christ and the Buddha. Each is a personification of a principle that informs our lives. St. Paul says, "I live now. Not I, but Christ in me." That means, "I am motivated by the Christ principle." The Buddhas say, "All things are Buddha things; all things are Buddha—you and me." St. Paul knew he was a Buddha thing, and he lived out of that center.

I read a very interesting little piece by Suzuki the other day. He was the Japanese philosopher who really introduced Zen thinking to our country. He died about twenty years ago, close to the age of ninety. In this article he was making a distinction between what he called "the Buddha nature in being" and "the Buddha nature experience." There's a huge difference. We are all manifestations of Buddha nature, so are the trees, so are the stones, so are all the animals. All life is a manifestation of this dynamic. Then, however, comes the consciousness and the realization that *you* are also of that Buddha nature, and that *you* are living out of that center. Now, that is exactly what St. Paul is speaking about in a different *folk inflection* from Suzuki.

There's a very amusing story of a little disciple who comes to his Master and says, "O Master, am I of the Buddha nature?"

And the Master says, "No, you are not."

"Well I've heard that all the stones, and all insects, and all the animals are manifestations of the Buddha nature—all beings. And I'm not?"

"Oh," said the Master. "It's true. All nature, all insects, all stones are manifestations of the Buddha nature. But not you."

"Why not me?"

"Because you're asking the question!"

What the Master was saying was that the disciple was putting himself up in his head and not experiencing it. He was not living his life out of that center.

There's a wonderful idea that's called "the Awakening of Faith," by which if you live as though you knew you were the Buddha nature then one day you'll know about it. You'll feel it moving through your life. Now, in Christianity that would be called the Christ nature. Except that our religion has separated us from the Christ nature because it is said to be peculiar to Jesus of Nazareth and no one else can identify himself with the Christ. So if someone says, "I am the Christ!" it's blasphemy and insanity. Whereas, if you can't say that, you haven't really understood your Christ nature at all. This is an important difference between these two religions. Christianity has been concretized in an historical character, and his life is not symbolic of what should happen to you.

I can remember Good Friday meditations. I was a good little Catholic boy, and between noon and three o'clock on Good Friday, we'd have meditations on the Crucifixion during which we were to think of the weight of Jesus' cross, and how our sins have weighed down the cross, and how we should ask for forgiveness, and all this kind of stuff, instead of realizing that we're all carrying our cross. The cross symbolizes the earthly body, and what Jesus was doing was going through the cross to the father and transcendence. That's why he returns Easter Sunday radiant. It's exactly the same motif as that of the Buddha seated, touching the earth, dismissing the Lord of Life, Death, Lust, and Duty. The Buddha has come to the realization of the spirit, and so it pours forth. This is the whole parable of myth—that you should become a vehicle of the radiance of the transcendent either by belonging to this community, which is itself a manifestation, or by realizing it in yourself. Our culture has lost it. We don't believe it.

Are you saying you're the Second Coming?

Everyone is the Second Coming as soon as one has the experience. You're it! Change the focus of your eyes. The central mountain is *everywhere*. *Is* everywhere. It is not *going to be* everywhere. It's here *now*. That's the real message of myth.

LIBRARY OF CONGRESS
CATALOGING-IN-PUBLICATION DATA

Campbell, Joseph, 1904–
[This business of the gods]
The way of myth: talking with
Joseph Campbell/Fraser Boa.
p.   cm. —(Shambhala pocket editions)
Originally published: Toronto: Windrose Films, 1989.
ISBN 1-57062-042-3 (pbk.: alk. paper)
1. Campbell, Joseph, 1904—Interviews.
2. Myth.   3. Religion.
4. Spiritual life.   I. Boa, Fraser, 1932–   .   II. Title.
III. Series.
BL304.C363   1994   94-6186
291.1′3—dc20   CIP

THE WAY OF MYTH
Talking with Joseph Campbell
by Fraser Boa

is based on the
documentary film series
This business of the gods . . .
featuring Joseph Campbell in
conversation with Fraser Boa
(8 half-hour 16 mm. films),
which is available for use in
classrooms and workshops.

Film series distributed by
Windrose Films Limited
P.O. Box 265, Station "Q", Toronto
Ontario M4T 2M1, Canada